POETRY BY CANADIAN WOMEN

Edited by Rosemary Sullivan

Toronto OXFORD UNIVERSITY PRESS 1989

For my sisters Patricia, Sharon, and Colleen

Oxford University Press, 70 Wynford Drive, Don Mills, Ontario, M3C 1J9

Toronto   Oxford   New York   Delhi   Bombay   Calcutta   Madras   Karachi
Petaling Jaya   Singapore   Hong Kong   Tokyo   Nairobi   Dar es Salaam
Cape Town   Melbourne   Auckland

and associated companies in
Berlin   Ibadan

CANADIAN CATALOGUING IN PUBLICATION DATA
Main entry under title:
Poetry by Canadian women

Includes index.
ISBN 0-19-540688-5

1. Canadian poetry (English)—Women authors.*
I. Sullivan, Rosemary.

PS8283.W6P64 1989   C811'.008'09287   C88-095288-1
L9841   PR9195.3.P64 1989

Cover painting by Matt Gould

CONTENTS

INTRODUCTION

> Masterpieces are not single and solitary births; they are the outcome of
> many years of thinking in common, of thinking by the body of the
> people, so that the experience of the mass is behind the single voice.
> Jane Austen should have laid a wreath upon the grave of Fanny Burney,
> and George Eliot done homage to the robust shade of Eliza Carter—
> the valiant woman who tied a bell to her bedstead in order that she
> might wake early and learn Greek.
>
> Virginia Woolf: A Room of One's Own

If one were to follow Virginia Woolf's advice, one would read this
anthology as a cumulative work, a single long poem created over one
and a half centuries by women poets writing in Canada. Behind the
eclectic generation of contemporary women writers is a cumulative
tradition of poets who might be thought of as facilitators, clearing a
space for future voices. One of the pleasures of editing this anthology
has been to identify these, since many voices have disappeared. Another
has been to trace the evolution in the concerns of women poets. To
those who, fearing ghettoization, resist the idea of collecting women's
writing under a single cover, one can only respond with Virginia
Woolf's insistence: we need the homage of memory, the catalytic
power of the retrospective glance.

This anthology begins in the early nineteenth century. In research-
ing archival material I found an unexpected number of women writers,
among them Sarah and Mary E. Herbert, Clotilda Jennings, Mrs R.
Leprohon, Mary Jane Katzmann, Agnes Marchar, and M.G. Currie.
But my criterion for selection was never purely historical. I wanted
poems that could sustain a modern reader's attention. The first such
poet I found was Margaret Blennerhasset. About her we know little
more than that she wrote under the alias 'A Lady', and was born in
Ireland. Many of her poems are frontier idylls—conventional tales of
lost happiness that sublimate actual historical events. She and her
husband had invested heavily in Aaron Burr's expedition to fight the
Spanish and conquer Mexico. When the expedition ended in disgrace,
they had had to abandon their mansion near Parkersburg, Virginia,
and flee to Canada. Though famous in her day for romantic narratives,
she had wit and a sharp tongue, and it is her poems written from an
almost feminist perspective that are still intriguing.

Often we condescend to history, especially where the historical
experience of women is concerned, assuming that economic and social
constraints on the lives of earlier generations meant that they could

never equal the independence and ambition of modern women. But the writers who follow Blennerhasset—Moodie, Yule, Crawford, Harrison, Blewett, Johnson—had interesting literary careers that they pursued single-mindedly. Moodie we know as the author of *Roughing it in the Bush*, that feisty manual warning prospective pioneers of the hazards of the Canadian wilderness. Harrison, also of Irish extraction, was a professional pianist and vocalist, and composed songs and an opera. An amateur anthropologist, she collected French Canadian folk songs that provided material for her poetry. Blewett began writing in her teens and eventually joined the staff of the Toronto *Globe*.

That there was a place for women in the new enterprise of founding a Canadian literature is clear: their names appear frequently in the half-dozen influential journals of the day. That they had to face condescension is also clear. In 1888 Sarah Jeannette Duncan complained that women weren't fairly represented in the conservative world of journalism: 'and we know what conservatism means in relation to the scope of women's work.' She counselled the 'divinest kind of patience'. Describing Pamelia Vining Yule's resignation as a teacher of English Art and Literature at Woodstock College, her biographer writes: 'she entered upon the greatest opportunity that can come to a woman, which is that of a homemaker' (1925). Like the work of their male contemporaries who earned the label 'The Confederation Poets', the literature these women produced remains most interesting for its anticipatory value: they pioneered a place for later women writers.

Any anthologist, but especially one whose focus is women writers, has to confront the question of what determines literary reputation. Why do some names survive rather than others when the objective criterion, the work, seems to be of equal merit? Where, for instance, is the name of Louise Morey Bowman in the history of Canadian Modernism? In the twenties we think of A.J.M. Smith and Frank Scott as the young Turks who championed Modernism in the pages of their iconoclastic student magazine *The McGill Fortnightly Review*. But the new poetics were being practised earlier than is generally realized, though it took the new 'movement' to galvanize attention. Thus Bowman disappeared. Her work deserves to be resurrected.

Most writers, at one point in their career, need the catalytic influence of other writers who share their concerns. There are exceptions, and often one mentor suffices, but that poetry is a dialogue with other writers, as well as with the self, is clear. P.K. Page came into her own as a poet when she joined the *Preview* poets and discovered the work of A.M. Klein. Margaret Avison initially found her sympathetic reader in Cid Corman of *Origin*. Adele Wiseman shared a youthful passion for fiction with Margaret Laurence. Perhaps Dorothy Livesay more than any other woman writer cultivated the relationship between writing and literary community. Wherever there was a new movement underway, there you would find Livesay: in the twenties with Leon Edel in Paris; in the thirties in Montreal working in the new theatre that focused on the depression; in the forties writing documentary verse-plays; in the early sixties in Africa; and in the late sixties on the West Coast studying linguistics and participating in the poetic movement called 'Projective Verse'. Livesay anticipated what is the most remarkable change among contemporary women writers: their sense of community; they know each other and gather strength from the sense of a shared enterprise.

It was in the forties and fifties that the first remarkable women poets began to publish: P.K. Page, whose capacity for metaphoric language no Canadian poet has equalled, and later Phyllis Webb, whose explorations in the realm of form, including her recent improvisations on the traditional Eastern ghazal, have signalled new directions for experiment. In the early sixties Margaret Avison appeared, followed by Gwendolyn MacEwen and Margaret Atwood. Each had a particular genius. No Canadian poet had yet demonstrated the linguistic sophistication of Avison in her pursuit of a personal metaphysic. MacEwen, with her interest in Greek and Egyptian mythology, demonstrated how the ordinary world could be made oracular and resonant. Atwood used an interest both in Canadian nationalism and in social mythology to create a new poetics: one in which an understanding of the relativism of perception forced us to see how we each invent our worlds. Her wit and clarity of image spawned a new generation of feminist writers. With their emergence, women poets were no longer simply a presence; they were at the vanguard of Canadian writing. By the seventies women writers had multiplied to such an extent that it became almost impossible to keep up with their numbers. And indeed the work of poets who should have been recognized much more widely, poets like Colleen Thibaudeau, Anne Szumigalski, Kay Smith, and Phyllis Gotlieb, is only beginning to get the attention it deserves.

To define what is happening in contemporary writing now, one must look not only to theme—clearly women writers can now lay claim to themes, whether sexual or political, that were unavailable to their predecessors—but also to craft. Paulette Jiles, one of the most interesting writers to surface recently, has a voice that has not been heard before: her images are superbly precise—bizarrely colloquial and yet formal; and the person she has created negotiates her way through a picaresque world that is at once both cynical and resonant.

Or there is Diana Hartog, who can sabotage romantic sentimentality with nostalgic humour by turning a folk echo on its head: 'Love's long bleached-blonde hair will always weep from a tower as we pull out fistfuls, shinnying up.' The assurance this humour demonstrates is a mark of the sophistication of the new poets.

That feminism and postmodernist technique have provided a new ethos for some of the poets can be seen in the work of Daphne Marlatt. Virginia Woolf said that the male declarative sentence couldn't carry the full meaning of women's minds. Marlatt concurs: 'our writing which we live inside of, is different from men's; not a tool . . . a pure instrument for getting a grip on the world . . . it contains menaces, traps, pitfalls.' 'To value the feminine', she believes, 'is the revolution of our times.' Poetry, which has evolved out of chant and song, must return to the ancient techniques of association—words evoking, provoking, nudging towards discovery. The experiments she initiated have had a profound effect on writers who have followed her, such as Lola Lemire Tostevin and Judith Fitzgerald, who have evolved their own precise idioms.

Other writers have sought space for the colloquial voice in poetry, so that themes formally debarred, particularly the politics of sexuality, can be articulated. Bronwen Wallace has turned to memories of anecdotal conversations from her rural background to create a loose and yet comprehensive prose line to sustain her ambling meditations on modern life. Erin Mouré, fiercely urban, has found a form, taut yet powerful, to contain her political denunciations of what we have managed to make of our world. Roo Borson and Mary di Michele have integrated both the lyric pressure of incisive image and a looser prose line in poems that lose nothing of the sensual resonance of their predecessors.

The seventies also saw the arrival in Canada of immigrant writers from widely different cultures whose work is only beginning to be generally known: writers from the Caribbean like Claire Harris, Marlene Nourbese Philip, and Dionne Brand, who have drawn on their roots, both political and linguistic, to invent a new poetics—creatively subversive in breaking down the narrowed boundaries of conventional language.

The world of women's writing has expanded, so that there is a new permission to be inclusive, whether in stylistic experiments or in theme. Much of this strength has come from the illumination that the woman writer is no longer an adjunct to the male literary world but stands in her own still centre, able to reach out to whatever is necessary to sustain the strength of her own creation. Phyllis Webb is insightful here. In the 'Preface' to *Wilson's Bowl* she responds to an inquiry about the predominance of male figures in her work:

> Some have suggested that these figures could be masks, personae, my animus, my male muse in many guises. I wonder and I think. I think that those interpretations are significant—I might even agree with them. They signify the domination of a male power culture in my educational and emotional formation so overpowering that I have, up to now, been denied access to inspiration from the female figures of my intellectual life, my heart, my imagination.

A split can be healed by the shock of recognition. That we write best when we learn to draw on our comprehensive identity, the creative self that Virginia Woolf called hermaphroditic, is, I think, demonstrated by the work of the poets in this anthology.

Furthermore, the profound impact that women's writing—for instance, the creative dialogue between George Bowering and Daphne Marlatt, Patrick Lane and Lorna Crozier—make it clear that when the artificial barriers are down, we are all the beneficiaries.

In editing this anthology my ambition has been to be as inclusive as possible. I have sought to demonstrate the full range of writing by Canadian women: from a historical perspective, and including diverse cultural backgrounds, temperaments, and styles. Constraints of space, however, have meant that some of the newer poets whose work deserves attention have been left out. For this I apologize. I would like to thank those writers who have assisted me in my work: P.K. Page for her suggestions as to writers I had overlooked, Richard Teleky for his editorial guidance, and Michael Ondaatje for his selection of my poetry. I hope the reader will find satisfaction from the cumulative impact of the anthology. 'Poems should echo and re-echo against one another. They should create resonance. They cannot live alone any more than we can,' as Robin Blaser once said. Perhaps the best justification for anthologies of poetry is that they cultivate the retrospective glance. There can be few literary satisfactions equal to hearing the multiple echoes of voices that, collectively, surface to make the present moment.

A note on dates: Dates following the poems refer to the date of first book publication. In some cases, where the poems have not been published in book form, the date refers to first magazine publication.

ACKNOWLEDGEMENTS

MARGARET ATWOOD Used by permission of Oxford University Press Canada: 'Death of a Young Son by Drowning', 'There is Only One of Everything' from *Selected Poems* © Margaret Atwood; and 'The Woman who could not live with her faulty heart', 'You Begin', 'Nothing', 'Earth', 'Notes Towards a Poem that Can Never Be Written' from *Selected Poems II* © Margaret Atwood 1986. MARGARET AVISON 'The Mourner', 'In a Season of Unemployment', 'July Man', 'Unspeakable' are reprinted from *The Dumbfounding* by Margaret Avison, by permission of W.W. Norton & Company, Inc. Copyright © 1966 by Margaret Avison. 'The World Still Needs', 'Snow', 'New Year's Poem', 'Voluptuaries and Others', 'The Swimmer's Moment' from *Winter Sun & The Dumbfounding* by Margaret Avison. Used by permission of the Canadian Publishers, McClelland and Stewart, Toronto. ROO BORSON 'Blackberries', 'Rain', 'Flying Low', 'St. Francis' from *The Whole Night Coming Home* by Roo Borson. Used by permission of the Canadian Publishers, McClelland and Stewart, Toronto. 'A Sad Device', 'Jacaranda' from *A Sad Device* used by permission of the author. MARILYN BOWERING 'Gains and Losses', 'The Origin of Species: Starting Point', 'The Sunday Before Winter' from *The Sunday Before Winter* (1984) by Marilyn Bowering. Used by permission of Stoddart Publishing Co. Limited, Don Mills, Canada. 'Well, it ain't no sin to take off your skin and dance around in your bones' from *Giving Back Diamonds*. Used by permission of Press Porcépic Limited. DIONNE BRAND 'Diary—The grenada crisis', 'Amelia', 'Amelia continued . . . ' from *Chronicles of the Hostile Sun* are used by permission of the author. ELIZABETH BREWSTER 'In Wellington, For Katherine Mansfield', 'Reading Old Poetry Notebooks' by Elizabeth Brewster are reprinted from *Selected Poems* by permission of Oberon Press. AUDREY ALEXANDRA BROWN 'Candles in the Glass' from *All Fools' Day* by Audrey Alexandra Brown. Copyright © The Ryerson Press, 1948. Reprinted by permission. SKYROS BRUCE All poems from *Kalala Poems*, 1972, Daylight Press, 1616 Charles Street, Vancouver, B.C. V5L 2T3, copyright held by Daylight Press (in trust for Skyros Bruce). JAN CONN All poems from *The Fabulous Disguise of Ourselves*. Used by permission of Véhicule Press. JENI COUZYN From 'Christmas in Africa', 'House of Changes' from *Life By Drowning* (Toronto: House of Anansi Press, 1983). Reprinted by permission. 'Cartography of the Subtle Heart' from *Life By Drowning* (Bloodaxe Books). LORNA CROZIER 'Poem About Nothing', 'We Call This Fear', 'Fishing in Air', 'The Morning of the Sad Women', *From* '"The Sex Life of Vegetable" Carrots, Cauliflower, Peas' from *The Garden Going On Without Us* by Lorna Crozier. Used by permission of the Canadian Publishers, McClelland and Stewart, Toronto. MARY DI MICHELE 'The Moon and the Salt Falts', from *Mumoso & Other Poems* Mosaic Press 1981. Used by permission. 'Orchids and Blood', 'Hunger' from *Immune to Gravity* by Mary di Michele. Used by permission of the Canadian Publishers, McClelland and Stewart, Toronto. 'Necessary Sugar' by Mary di Michele is reprinted from *Necessary Sugar* by permission of Oberon Press. GWLADYS DOWNES 'On the Sundeck', 'Stone Garden with Wasp', 'Flotsam at

Rose Point' are reprinted by permission of the author. 'Cannibal Speech' from *Out of the Violent Dark* by Gwladys Downes, Sono Nis Press, Victoria, B.C., 1978. Used by permission. JUDITH FITZGERALD All poems from *Diary of Desire*. Used by permission of Black Moss Press. GAIL FOX 'Cartoons' by Gail Fox is reprinted from *God's Odd Look* and 'Portrait' by Gail Fox is reprinted from *In Search of Living Things* by permission of Oberon Press. SUSAN GLICKMAN 'America' from *The Power of Move* used by permission of Véhicule Press. All other poems used by permission of the author. PHYLLIS GOTLIEB All poems used by permission of the author. ELIZABETH GOURLAY 'Poems for a Poet Friend' unpublished. All other poems from *Motions, Dreams & Aberrations* (1969). Used by permission of the author. KRISTJANA GUNNARS 'milky way vegetation II' from *The Night Workers of Ragnarok*. Used by permission of Press Porcépic Limited. All other poems used by permission of the author. CLAIRE HARRIS All poems from *Travelling to Find a Remedy*. Used by permission of Goose Lane Editions. DIANA HARTOG All poems reprinted by permission of the author. PAULETTE JILES 'Paper Matches', 'Flying Lesson', 'The Mystic', 'Living Alone' from *Celestial Navigation* by Paulette Jiles. Used by permission of the Canadian Publishers, McClelland and Stewart, Toronto. 'Waterloo Express', 'Dallas', 'Lanterns' used by permission of the author. JANICE KULYK KEEFER All poems used by permission of the author. JOY KOGAWA 'Ancestors' Graves in Kurakawa', 'Day of the Bride', and 'Hangnail' from *A Choice of Dreams* by Joy Kogawa. Used by permission of the Canadian Publishers, McClelland and Stewart, Toronto. 'If Your Mirror Breaks' from *Woman in the Woods* Mosaic Press 1985. Used by permission. DOROTHY LIVESAY All poems reprinted by permission of the author. PAT LOWTHER All poems used by permission from *A Stone Diary* © Oxford University Press (Canada) 1977. GWENDOLYN MACEWEN 'Water', 'The Desert', 'Absolute Room', 'Thunder-Song' from *The T.E. Lawrence Poems* by Gwendolyn MacEwen. Published 1982, second printing 1983 by Mosaic Press. Reprinted by permission. 'The Grand Dance', from *Afterwords* by Gwendolyn MacEwen. Used by permission of the Canadian Publishers, McClelland and Stewart, Toronto. 'The White Horse', 'A Breakfast for Barbarians', 'The Discovery', 'Dark Pines Under Water' from *Magic Animals* (1984) by Gwendolyn MacEwen. Reprinted by permission of Stoddart Publishing Co. Limited, Don Mills, Canada. JAY MACPHERSON All poems used by permission from *Poems Twice Told* © Oxford University Press Canada 1981. DAPHNE MARLATT Used by permission of the author: 'Femina' from *Vancouver Poems*; 'Rings. iii' from *What Matters*; 'Avebury awi-spek. winged from buried (egg' from *How Hug a Stone*; 'Prairie', 'Kore' from *Touch To My Tongue*. ANNE MARRIOTT 'Prairie Graveyard', 'Port Renfrew' from *The Circular Coast* Mosaic Press 1980. Used by permission. 'July 25', 'Story from Utah' from *Letters From Some Island* Mosaic Press 1985. Used by permission. ANNE MICHAELS All poems reprinted by permission of the author. LUCY MAUD MONTGOMERY 'The Test', 'I Feel (Vers Libre)', 'To My Enemy' from *The Poetry of Lucy Maud Montgomery*. Used by permission of Fitzhenry & Whiteside. ERIN MOURÉ 'Vision of a Woman Hit by a Bird', 'Philosophy of Language', 'Glow', 'Gale Force' from *Domestic Fuel* (Toronto, House of

Anansi Press, 1985). Reprinted by permission. 'Aspen', 'The Producers' from *Furious* (Toronto, House of Anansi Press, 1988). Reprinted by permission. RONA MURRAY All poems reprinted by permission of the author. SUSAN MUSGRAVE Used by permission of the Canadian Publishers, McClelland and Stewart, Toronto: 'Entrance of the Celebrant' from *Tarts & Muggers* by Susan Musgrave; and 'The Moon is Upside Down in the Sky', 'Cocktails at the Mausoleum', 'I Do Not Know If Things That Happen Can Be Said To Come to Pass or Only to Happen' from *Cocktails at the Mausoleum* by Susan Musgrave. P.K. PAGE All poems reprinted by permission of the author. MARLENE NOURBESE PHILIP Reprinted by permission of the author. DOROTHY ROBERTS All poems reprinted by permission of the author. ROBYN SARAH All poems reprinted by permission of the author. LIBBY SCHEIER 'Penises. I', 'Women' reprinted by permission of the author. 'Five Meditations on Jungles', 'There Is No Such Thing As Silence' from *The Larger Life*. Used by permission of Black Moss Press. CAROLYN SMART 'Telling Lies' and 'Flying' by Carolyn Smart are reprinted from *Stoning the Moon* by permission of Oberon Press. ELIZABETH SMART 'Rose Died', 'The Muse: His & Hers' from *In the Meantime* (1984). Used by permission of Deneau Publishers & Company Ltd. KAY SMITH All poems reprinted from *The Bright Particulars* by permission of the author. ROSEMARY SULLIVAN All poems used by permission of the author. ANNE SZUMIGALSKI All poems from *Dogstone* by Anne Szumigalski. Used by permission of Fifth House Publishers. SHARON THESEN All poems used by permission of the author. COLLEEN THIBAUDEAU All poems used by permission of the author. LOLA LEMIRE TOSTEVIN Used by permission of the author. RHEA TREGEGOV All poems used by permission of the author. KATE VAN DUSEN All poems used by permission of the author. MIRIAM WADDINGTON All poems reprinted from *Collected Poems* © Miriam Waddington, by permission of Oxford University Press. BRONWEN WALLACE 'Melons at the Speed of Light', 'Common Magic' by Bronwen Wallace are reprinted from *Common Magic* by permission of Oberon Press. 'Joseph MacLeod Daffodils' from *The Stubborn Particulars of Grace* by Bronwen Wallace. Used by permission of the Canadian Publishers, McClelland and Stewart, Toronto. PHYLLIS WEBB All poems used by permission of the author. ANNE WILKINSON All poems used by permission of Alan Wilkinson. ADELE WISEMAN All poems used by permission of the author.

MARGARET BLENNERHASSET
(alias A Lady)
1778?–1842

Sir Walter Raleigh's Advice to His Son on the Subject of Matrimony.

Since Horace sung, and long before,
Has woman felt man's tyrant power.
'False' and 'fickle' are slight charges
When disappointed man enlarges,
On weak woman's many failings,
While *he*, quite just in all his railings,
For truth and constancy renoun'd,
Her perfect contrast would be found.
But,—just by way of illustration,
A wise man once, in lofty station,
Bequeathed his son a legacy
Of good advice, to keep him free
From all the turmoil care and strife
That wait upon a wedded life.

'My son,' he said, 'love on—but think
'Tis better far to love than *link*
'Real thy years,—bethink thee when
'A sucking child, what thou didst then:
'—Didst love thy wet-nurse with affection
'Till wean'd thou mad'st a new election,
'Thy dry-nurse then suffic'd thy heart,
'Quite willing from the first to part.
'To boyhood grown say didst thou grieve,
'—Thy second favorite to leave?
'—The fate of these thy first two loves,
('Their care no longer needful) proves
'That so 'twill be in after years,
'When beauty thy young heart ensnares
'With ardour first the flame to burn
'And all to one thy liking turn,
'A second will that first supplant,
'Then for a third thy heart will pant,
'And so 'twill be with many more,
'From one—two—three—up to a score.'

Thus sung (or said) Sir Walter Raleigh,
   A knight for crafty wisdom fam'd;
But sailors' hearts are somewhat squally,
   To dove-like constancy not tam'd.

Thus men, of woman's power jealous,
   Endeav'ring to degrade the fair,
(For their *prerogative* quite zealous)
   Asperse what they should guard with care.

Blind to her charms her faults they chide,
   Nor give to nature's weakness lenience:
Their *wife* is but the slave of pride,
   Or sort of household-stuff convenience.

A wretched life we must confess,
   The Indian has a better mode
His Squaw—his slave,—no more—nor less,—
   To pound his corn—to lug his load.

1824

SUSANNA MOODIE
1803–1885

The Nautical Philosophers

A Sketch from Life.

Dear merry reader, did you ever hear,
   Whilst travelling on the world's wide beaten road,
The curious reasoning and opinions queer,
   Of men, who never in their lives bestowed
One hour on study,—whose existence seems
   A thing of course, a practical delusion;
A day of frowning clouds, and sunny gleams,
   Of pain and pleasure mixed in strange confusion,
Who feel they move and breathe, they know not why—
   Are born to eat, and drink, and sleep and die.

Who judge internal from external things,
   And will not look one inch beyond their nose;
Who yet believe that angel forms have wings,

Because such shapes some dirty sign post shows,
Though they such birds on earth have never seen,
    The painter must have known the wondrous vision,
Or how could he array in blue and green,
    The grinning ape that wakens arts' derision;
Yet seems to these deluded sons of sin,
    The etherial type of spirits, rum and gin.

It was my chance upon a summer's day,
    Within a close packed omnibus, to meet
Two of these learned Athenians, who betray
    Their folly at each turning of the street;
Who grin and stare, and talk in accents loud,
    Stunning to right and left, each luckless neighbour,
To draw the attention of the gaping crowd
    To their own ignorant and rude behaviour,
Of taxes, kings, and ministers, they chatter,
    And seldom know one word about the matter.

My fellow travellers were a grade above
    The hungry loafer, ever bawling treason:
Though constantly they sought their oar to shove
    In each discourse, without a rhyme or reason;
Giving unasked advice, opinions, broaching,
    Making remarks, unawed by time or place,
On each man's mental manor boldly poaching,
    Then laughing in the angry listener's face—
Two of old Neptune's rough, untutored sons,
    Cracking coarse jokes, and murdering viler puns.

Stern time had furrowed with his iron plough,
    The elder seaman's tanned and homely face,
Tracing strange hieroglyphics on a brow,
    Peculiar to his bold amphibious race,
Broad and erect, as though the sun and storm
    Against its native strength their force had tried,
Failing to bend the stout herculean form,
    That wind and wave from boyhood had defied,—
A child in knowledge, though his hairs were white,
    Called by his country not to think, but fight.

Such was the elder of the twain. His mate
    A youth, with scarce the down upon his chin,

With ruddy cheeks and merry brow elate,
    And oh, what depths of mischief lurked within
The clear, blue, roguish, laughter-loving eye,
    From right to left, in quick succession glancing,
Nodding to each fair damsel passing by,
    Giving the lie to his own wild romancing,
By the shrewd covert look, which told each man,
    You may believe me, messmate—if you can.

Such were the twain, whose portraits I would draw,
    Digressing sadly in my rambling rhyme,
But entertained with all I heard and saw,
    Their features did impress me at the time,
And by my sex protected, I enjoyed
    Their varied traits of character to mark,
And the wild reckless nonsense that annoyed
    Our living cargo, woke in me no spark
Of vain resentment, for the men were but
    What nature from the rugged block had cut.

At Islington we made a sudden pause—
    Which threw our seamen nose and knees together,
And after laughing loudly at the cause,
    They turned their conversation on the weather;
'For July, Jack, methinks 'tis wondrous cold,
    These wet, dull summers, scarce can warm a flea;
In my young days—for now I'm growing old—
    The dog-days were as hot as days could be;
I've gathered cherries, red and ripe in May,
    And helped the lassies ted the new-mown hay.

'Each year, methinks the sun's been growing dimmer,
    Winking upon us with a drowsy eye,
As though he scorned upon the earth to glimmer,
    Reserving all his good looks for the sky;
The red-faced varlet!—I should like to know
    What we have done to merit his disdain;
We soon shall see in summer frost and snow,
    For ever drench'd with this eternal rain;
A ship might sail along this street of mud,
    As well as did the ark on Noah's flood!'

'I never knew a letter in the book,'
    Returned his comrade, with a waggish leer;
'Nor climbed a ladder in the skies to look,
    But I can tell the cause, though some may sneer.
The sun do ye see, is sinking fast in years,
    And age, you know, the warmest blood will chill,
As time creeps on, more dull his lamp appears,
    And so 'twill be, till nature's pulse stands still;
This is the reason why his rays are cold;
    The sun, like you, old boy! is growing old!'

1847

The Future Flower

The future flower lies folded in the bud—
Its beauty, colour, fragrance, graceful form,
Carefully shrouded in that tiny cell;
Till time and circumstance, and sun and shower.
Expand the embryo blossom—and its bursts
Its narrow cerements, lifts its blushing head,
Rejoicing in the light and dew of heaven.
But if the canker-worm lies coil'd around
The heart o' the bud, the summer sun and dew
Visit in vain the sear'd and blighted flower.

1852

O Can You Leave Your Native Land?

(For Music.)

O can you leave your native land,
    An exile's bride to be;
Your mother's home and cheerful hearth
    To tempt the main with me—
Across the wide and stormy sea
    To trace our foaming track,
And know the wave that heaves us on
    Will never bear us back?

And can you in Canadian wood
    With me the harvest bind,
Nor feel one lingering sad regret
    For all you leave behind!
Can those dear hands, unused to toil,
    The woodman's wants supply,
Nor shrink beneath the chilly blast
    When wintry storms are nigh?

Amid the shades of forests dark,
    Our loved isle will appear
An Eden, whose delicious bloom
    Will make the wild more drear—
And you in solitude will weep
    O'er scenes belov'd in vain,
And pine away your life to view
    Once more your native plain!

Then pause, dear girl, ere those fond lips
    Your wanderer's fate decide;
My spirit spurns the selfish wish—
    You must not be my bride—
But oh, that smile—those tearful eyes
    My firmer purpose move—
Our hearts are one—and we will dare
    All perils thus to love.

1864

PAMELIA VINING YULE
1825–1897

Littlewit and Loftus

John Littlewit, friends, was a *credulous* man,
    In the good time long ago,
Ere men had gone wild o'er the latter-day dream
Of turning the world upside down with steam,
Or of chaining the lightning down to a wire,
And making it talk with its tongue of fire.

He was perfectly sure that the world stood still,
    And the sun and moon went round;—
He believed in fairies, and goblins ill,
And witches that rode over vale and hill
On wicked broom-sticks, studying still
    Mischief and craft profound.

'What a fool was John Littlewit!' somebody cries;—
    Nay, friend, not so fast, if you please!
  A humble man was John Littlewit—
    A gentle, loving man;
He clothed the needy, the hungry fed,
Pitied the erring, the faltering led,
Joyed with the joyous, wept with the sad,
Made the heart of the widow and orphan glad,
And never left for the lowliest one
An act of kindness and love undone;—
  And when he died, we may well believe
    God's blessed angels bore
John Littlewit's peaceful soul away
To the beautiful Heaven for which we pray,
Where the tree of knowledge blooms for aye,
    And ignorance plagues no more.

Squire Loftus, friends, was a *cultured* man,
    You knew him—so did I:
He had studied the 'Sciences' through and through,
Had forgotten far more than the ancients knew,
    Yet still retained enough
To demonstrate clearly that all the old,
Good, practical Bible-truths we hold
    Are delusions, nonsense, stuff!

He could show that the earth had begun to grow
Millions and millions of ages ago;
That men had developed up and out
From something Moses knew nothing about;—
Held with Pope that all are but parts of a whole,
Whose body is Nature, and God its Soul;—
And, since *he* was a part of that same great whole,
Then the soul of all Nature was also his soul;—
Or, more plainly—to be not obscure or dim—

That God had *developed Himself* in him:—
That what is called *Sin* in mankind, is not so,
But is just *misdirection*, all owing, you know,
To defectiveness either of body or brain,
Or both, which the soul is not thought to retain;—
In the body it acts as it *must*, but that dead
All stain from the innocent soul will have fled!

'How wise was Squire Loftus!' there's somebody cries;—
    Nay, friend, not so fast, if you please;
His wisdom was that of the self-deceived fool
Who quits the clear fount for the foul, stagnant pool,
Who puts out his eyes lest the light he descry,
Then shouts 'mid the gloom 'how clear-sighted am I!'
Who turns from the glorious fountain of Day,
To follow the wild *ignis fatuus'* ray
Through quagmire and swamp, ever farther astray,
    With every step that he takes.

But he died as he lived; and the desolate night
He had courted and loved better far than the light,
Grew more and more dark, till he passed from our sight,
    And what shall I say of him more?—
Give me rather John Littlewit's questionless faith,
To illume my lone path through the valley of death—
The arm that he leaned on, the mansion of light
That burst through the gloom on his kindling sight,
    And I'll leave the poor sceptic his lore!—
Let me know only this—*I was lost and undone,*
But am saved by the blood of the Crucified One,
    And I'm *wise* although knowing no more!

1881

ISABELLA VALANCY CRAWFORD
1850–1887

The Camp of Souls

My white canoe, like the silvery air
    O'er the River of Death that darkly rolls
When the moons of the world are round and fair,
    I paddle back from the 'Camp of Souls'.

When the wishton-wish in the low swamp grieves
Come the dark plumes of red 'Singing Leaves'.

Two hundred times have the moons of spring
    Rolled over the bright bay's azure breath
Since they decked me with plumes of an eagle's wing,
    And painted my face with the 'paint of death',
And from their pipes o'er my corpse there broke
The solemn rings of the blue 'last smoke'.

Two hundred times have the wintry moons
    Wrapped the dead earth in a blanket white;
Two hundred times have the wild sky loons
    Shrieked in the flush of the golden light
Of the first sweet dawn, when the summer weaves
Her dusky wigwam of perfect leaves.

Two hundred moons of the falling leaf
    Since they laid my bow in my dead right hand
And chanted above me the 'song of grief'
    As I took my way to the spirit land;
Yet when the swallow the blue air cleaves
Come the dark plumes of red 'Singing Leaves'.

White are the wigwams in that far camp,
    And the star-eyed deer on the plains are found;
No bitter marshes or tangled swamp
    In the Manitou's happy hunting-ground!
And the moon of summer forever rolls
Above the red men in their 'Camp of Souls'.

Blue are its lakes as the wild dove's breast,
    And their murmurs soft as her gentle note;
As the calm, large stars in the deep sky rest,
    The yellow lilies upon them float;
And canoes, like flakes of the silvery snow,
Thro' the tall, rustling rice-beds come and go.

Green are its forests; no warrior wind
    Rushes on war trail the dusk grove through,
With leaf-scalps of tall trees mourning behind;
    But South Wind, heart friend of Great Manitou,
When ferns and leaves with cool dews are wet,
Blows flowery breaths from his red calumet.

Never upon them the white frosts lie,
   Nor glow their green boughs with the 'paint of death';
Manitou smiles in the crystal sky,
   Close breathing above them His life-strong breath;
And He speaks no more in fierce thunder sound,
So near is His happy hunting-ground.

Yet often I love, in my white canoe,
   To come to the forests and camps of earth:
'Twas there death's black arrow pierced me through;
   'Twas there my red-browed mother gave me birth;
There I, in the light of a young man's dawn,
Won the lily heart of dusk 'Springing Fawn'.

And love is a cord woven out of life,
   And dyed in the red of the living heart;
And time is the hunter's rusty knife,
   That cannot cut the red strands apart:
And I sail from the spirit shore to scan
Where the weaving of that strong cord began.

But I may not come with a giftless hand,
   So richly I pile, in my white canoe,
Flowers that bloom in the spirit land,
   Immortal smiles of Great Manitou.
When I paddle back to the shores of earth
I scatter them over the white man's hearth.

For love is the breath of the soul set free;
   So I cross the river that darkly rolls,
That my spirit may whisper soft to thee
   Of *thine* who wait in the 'Camp of Souls'.
When the bright day laughs, or the wan night grieves,
Come the dusky plumes of red 'Singing Leaves'.

1880

The City Tree

I stand within the stony, arid town,
   I gaze forever on the narrow street,

I hear forever passing up and down
  The ceaseless tramp of feet.

I know no brotherhood with far-locked woods,
  Where branches bourgeon from a kindred sap,
Where o'er mossed roots, in cool, green solitudes,
  Small silver brooklets lap.

No emerald vines creep wistfully to me
  And lay their tender fingers on my bark;
High may I toss my boughs, yet never see
  Dawn's first most glorious spark.

When to and fro my branches wave and sway,
  Answ'ring the feeble wind that faintly calls,
They kiss no kindred boughs, but touch alway
  The stones of climbing walls.

My heart is never pierced with song of bird;
  My leaves know nothing of that glad unrest
Which makes a flutter in the still woods heard
  When wild birds build a nest.

There never glance the eyes of violets up,
  Blue, into the deep splendour of my green;
Nor falls the sunlight to the primrose cup
  My quivering leaves between.

Not mine, not mine to turn from soft delight
  Of woodbine breathings, honey sweet and warm;
With kin embattled rear my glorious height
  To greet the coming storm!

Not mine to watch across the free, broad plains
  The whirl of stormy cohorts sweeping fast,
The level silver lances of great rains
  Blown onward by the blast!

Not mine the clamouring tempest to defy,
  Tossing the proud crest of my dusky leaves—
Defender of small flowers that trembling lie
  Against my barky greaves!

Not mine to watch the wild swan drift above,
   Balanced on wings that could not choose between
The wooing sky, blue as the eye of love,
   And my own tender green!

And yet my branches spread, a kingly sight,
   In the close prison of the drooping air:
When sun-vexed noons are at their fiery height
   My shade is broad, and there

Come city toilers, who their hour of ease
   Weave out to precious seconds as they lie
Pillowed on horny hands, to hear the breeze
   Through my great branches die.

I see no flowers, but as the children race
   With noise and clamour through the dusty street,
I see the bud of many an angel face,
   I hear their merry feet.

No violets look up, but, shy and grave,
   The children pause and lift their crystal eyes
To where my emerald branches call and wave
   As to the mystic skies.

1880

From *Gisli the Chieftain*

THE SONG OF THE ARROW

What know I,
As I bite the blue veins of the throbbing sky,
To the quarry's breast,
Hot from the sides of the sleek, smooth nest?

What know I
Of the will of the tense bow from which I fly?
What the need or jest
That feathers my flight to its bloody rest?

What know I
Of the will of the bow that speeds me on high?

What doth the shrill bow
Of the hand on its singing soul-string know?

Flame-swift speed I,
And the dove and the eagle shriek out and die.
Whence comes my sharp zest
For the heart of the quarry? The gods know best.

Deep pierced the red gaze of the eagle
The breast of a cygnet below him.
Beneath his dun wing from the eastward
Shrill chanted the long shaft of Gisli;

Beneath his dun wing from the westward
A shaft shook that laughed in its biting—
Met in the fierce breast of the eagle
The arrows of Gisli and Brynhild.

1884

SUSIE FRANCES HARRISON
(alias Seranus)
1859–1935

Catharine Plouffe

This grey-haired spinster, Catharine Plouffe—
    Observe her, a contrast to convent chits,
At her spinning wheel, in the room in the roof.

Yet there are those who believe that the hoof
    Of a horse is nightly heard as she knits—
This grey-haired spinster, Catharine Plouffe—

Stockings of fabulous warp and woof,
    And that old Benedict's black pipe she permits
At her spinning wheel, in the room in the roof,

For thirty years. So the gossip. A proof
    Of her constant heart? Nay. No one twits
This grey-haired spinster, Catharine Plouffe;

The neighbours respect her, but hold aloof,
    Admiring her back as she steadily sits
At her spinning wheel, in her room in the roof.

Will they ever marry? Just ask her. Pouf!
    She would like you to know she's not lost her wits—
This grey-haired spinster, Catharine Plouffe,
At her spinning wheel, in her room in the roof.

1891

Les Chantiers

For know, my girl, there is always the axe
    Ready at hand in this latitude,
And how it stings and bites and hacks

When Alphonse the sturdy trees attacks!
    So fear, child, to cross him, or play the prude,
For know, my girl, there is always the axe.

See! It shines even now as his hands relax
    Their grip with a dread desire imbued,
And how it stings and bites and hacks,

And how it rips and cuts and cracks—
    Perhaps—in his brain as the foe is pursued!
For know, my girl, there is always the axe.

The giant boles in the forest tracks
    Stagger, soul-smitten, when afar it is viewed,
And how it stings and bites and hacks!

Then how, Madelon, should its fearful thwacks
    A slender lad like your own elude?
For know, my girl, there is always the axe,
And how it stings! and bites! and hacks!

1891

November

These are the days that try us; these the hours
That find, or leave us, cowards—doubters of Heaven,
Sceptics of self, and riddled through with vain
Blind questionings as to Deity. Mute, we scan
The sky, the barren, wan, the drab, dull sky,
And mark it utterly blank. Whereas, a fool,
The flippant fungoid growth of modern mode,
Uncapped, unbelled, unshorn, but still a fool,
Fate at his fingers' ends, and Cause in tow,
Or, wiser, say, the Yorick of his age,
The Touchstone of his period, would forecast
Better than us, the film and foam of rose
That yet may float upon the eastern grays
At dawn to-morrow.
                        Still, and if we could,
We would not change our gloom for glibness, lose
Our wonder in our faith.   We are not worse
Than those in whom the myth was strongest, those
In whom first awe lived longest, those who found
—Dear Pagans—gods in fountain, flood and flower.
Sometimes the old Hellenic base stirs, lives
Within us, and we thrill to branch and beam
When walking where the aureoled autumn sun
Looms golden through the chestnuts. But to-day
When sodden leaves are merged in melting mire,
And garden-plots lie pilfered, and the vines
Are strings of tangled rigging reft of green,
Crude harps whereon the winter wind shall play
His bitter music—on a day like this,
We, harboring no Hellenic images, stand
In apathy mute before our window pane,
And muse upon the blankness.   Then, O, then,
If ever, should we thank our God for those
Rare spirits who have testified in faith
Of such a world as this, and straight we pray
For such an eye as Wordsworth's, he who saw
System in anarchy, progress in ruin, peace
In devastation.   Duty was his star—
May it be ours—this Star the Preacher missed.

1891

JEAN BLEWETT
1862–1934

The Cornflower

The day she came we were planting corn,
  The west eighty-acre field,—
These prairie farms are great for size,
  And they're sometimes great for yield.

'The new school-ma'am is up to the house',
  The chore-boy called out to me;
I went in wishing anyone else
  Had been put in chief trustee.

I was to question that girl, you see,
  Of the things she ought to know;
As for these same things, I knew right well
  I'd forgot them long ago.

I hadn't kept track of women's ways,
  'Bout all I knew of the sex
Was that they were mighty hard to please,
  And easy enough to vex.

My sister Mary, who ruled my house—
  And me—with an iron hand,
Was all the woman I knew real well—
  Her I didn't understand.

But I'd no call to grumble at fate,
  Fifty, well off, and unwed;
Young as a lad in spite of the dust
  Old Time had thrown on my head.

I engaged the school-ma'am on the spot,
  And the reason, I surmise,
Was this, she didn't giggle or blush,
  But looked me fair in the eyes.

The planting over, why, every lad
  In a space of ten good mile
Was off for the school with a sudden zeal
  That made all us old folks smile.

How she took to our wide prairie
  After towns with narrow streets!
To watch that west eighty-acre field
  Was one of her queer conceits.

'You planted that corn the day I came',
  She said, 'and I love to go
And watch the sun-mother kiss and coax
  Each slim green stalk to grow.'

I called her 'Cornflower' when she took
  To wearing 'em in her belt.
The young chaps were all in love with her—
  And I knew just how they felt.

Oh, I tell you that was a summer,
  Such sunshine, such dew, such rain;
Never saw crops grow so in my life—
  Don't expect I will again.

To watch that west eighty-acre field,
  When the fall came clear and cold,
Was something like a sermon to me—
  Made me think of streets of gold.

But about that time the new school-ma'am
  Had words with the first trustee,
A scholar had taken the fever
  And she was for blaming *me*.

That schoolhouse should be raised from the ground—
  Grave reason there for alarm;
A new coat of plaster be put on
  That the children be kept warm.

A well—a good one—should take the place
  Of the deathtrap that was there.
'This should all be done at once,' she said.
  Cost five hundred dollars clear!

I told her I couldn't think of it,
  But, when all my work was through,
If the taxes came in middling good,
  I would see what I could do.

'Remember you're only the steward,'
    She said, 'of your acres broad,
And that the cry of a little child
    Goes straight to the ears of God.'

I remarked that it wasn't her place
    To dictate to the trustee,
And Cornflower lifted her eyes of blue
    And *looked* what she thought of me.

That night as we came up from the fields,
    And talked of the threatened frost,
The chore-boy called out, half pleased, half scared:
    'The school-ma'am's got herself lost.'

I turned me about and spoke no word;
    I'd find her and let her see
I held no spite 'gainst a wayward girl
    For lecturing a trustee.

For I knew before I found the knot
    Of ribbon that she had worn,
That somehow Betty had lost her way
    In the forest of ripened corn.

The sun went down and left the world
    Beautiful, happy and good;
True, the girl and myself had quarrelled,
    But when I found her and stood

With silver stars mistily shining
    Through the deep blue of the skies,
Heard somebody sob like a baby,
    Saw tears in somebody's eyes.

Why, I just whispered, 'Betty, Betty',
    Then whispered 'Betty' some more;
Not another word did I utter—
    I'll stick to this o'er and o'er.

You needn't ask me to explain, friends,
    I don't know how 'twas myself,

That first 'Betty' said I was ashamed
  Of my greedy love of pelf.

The second one told her I'd be glad
  To raise the old schoolhouse up,
And be in haste to put down a well,
  With a pump and drinking cup.

The third 'Betty' told her I would act
  A higher and nobler part;
The fourth 'Betty' told her I loved her—
  Loved her with all my heart.

'Ah, well! there's no fool like an old fool,'
  Was what sister Mary said;
'No fool in the world like an old fool,
  You'll find that out, brother Ned.'

'Mary,' I said, 'there's a better thing
  Than land, or dollar, or dime;
If being in love is being a fool
  Here's one till the end of time.'

I should think so, I'm a married man
  Four years come this Christmastide,
And autumn now is flinging her gold
  O'er the fields on every side.

My wife called out as I drove the cows
  To the pasture-field this morn,
'Ned, please go look for your son and heir,
  He toddled off in the corn.'

And sister Mary must make a joke;
  'Go find him at once,' said she,
'You know to get lost in a field of corn
  Runs in that boy's family.'

1906

E. PAULINE JOHNSON
1861–1913

Ojistoh

I am Ojistoh, I am she, the wife
Of him whose name breathes bravery and life
And courage to the tribe that calls him chief.
I am Ojistoh, his white star, and he
Is land, and lake, and sky—and soul to me.

Ah! but they hated him, those Huron braves,
Him who had flung their warriors into graves,
Him who had crushed them underneath his heel,
Whose arm was iron, and whose heart was steel
To all—save me, Ojistoh, chosen wife
Of my great Mohawk, white star of his life.

Ah! but they hated him, and councilled long
With subtle witchcraft how to work him wrong;
How to avenge their dead, and strike him where
His pride was highest, and his fame most fair.
Their hearts grew weak as women at his name:
They dared no war-path since my Mohawk came
With ashen bow, and flinten arrow-head
To pierce their craven bodies; but their dead
Must be avenged. Avenged? They dared not walk
In day and meet his deadly tomahawk;
They dared not face his fearless scalping knife;
So—Niyoh!*—then they thought of me, his wife.

O! evil, evil face of them they sent
With evil Huron speech: 'Would I consent
To take of wealth? be queen of all their tribe?
Have wampum ermine?' Back I flung the bribe
Into their teeth, and said, 'While I have life
Know this—Ojistoh is the Mohawk's wife.'

Wah! how we struggled! But their arms were strong.
They flung me on their pony's back, with thong
Round ankle, wrist, and shoulder. Then upleapt
The one I hated most: his eye he swept

*God, in the Mohawk language.

Over my misery, and sneering said,
'Thus, fair Ojistoh, we avenge our dead.'

And we two rode, rode as a sea wind-chased,
I, bound with buckskin to his hated waist,
He, sneering, laughing, jeering, while he lashed
The horse to foam, as on and on we dashed.
Plunging through creek and river, bush and trail,
On, on we galloped like a northern gale.
At last, his distant Huron fires aflame
We saw, and nearer, nearer still we came.

I, bound behind him in the captive's place,
Scarcely could see the outline of his face.
I smiled, and laid my cheek against his back:
'Loose thou my hands,' I said. 'This pace let slack.
Forget we now that thou and I are foes.
I like thee well, and wish to clasp thee close;
I like the courage of thine eye and brow;
I like thee better than my Mohawk now.'

He cut the cords; we ceased our maddened haste
I wound my arms about his tawny waist;
My hand crept up the buckskin of his belt;
His knife hilt in my burning palm I felt;
One hand caressed his cheek, the other drew
The weapon softly—'I love you, love you,'
I whispered, 'love you as my life.'
And—buried in his back his scalping knife.

Ha! how I rode, rode as a sea wind-chased,
Mad with sudden freedom, mad with haste,
Back to my Mohawk and my home. I lashed
That horse to foam, as on and on I dashed.
Plunging thro' creek and river, bush and trail,
On, on I galloped like a northern gale.
And then my distant Mohawk's fires aflame
I saw, as nearer, nearer still I came,
My hands all wet, stained with a life's red dye,
But pure my soul, pure as those stars on high—
'My Mohawk's pure white star, Ojistoh, still am I.'

1912

The Corn Husker

Hard by the Indian lodges, where the bush
  Breaks in a clearing, through ill-fashioned fields,
She comes to labour, when the first still hush
  Of autumn follows large and recent yields.

Age in her fingers, hunger in her face,
  Her shoulders stooped with weight of work and years,
But rich in tawny colouring of her race,
  She comes a-field to strip the purple ears.

And all her thoughts are with the days gone by,
  Ere might's injustice banished from their lands
Her people, that to-day unheeded lie,
  Like the dead husks that rustle through her hands.

1912

Wolverine

'Yes, sir, it's quite a story, though you won't believe it's true,
But such things happened often when I lived beyond the Soo.'
And the trapper tilted back his chair and filled his pipe anew.

'I ain't thought of it neither fer this many 'n many a day,
Although it used to haunt me in the years that's slid away;
The years I spent a-trappin' for the good old Hudson's Bay.

'Wild? You bet, 'twas wild then, an' few an' far between
The squatters' shacks, for whites was scarce as furs when things is
      green,
An' only reds an' 'Hudson's' men was all the folk I seen.

'No. Them old Indyans ain't so bad, not if you treat 'em square.
Why, I lived in amongst 'em all the winters I was there,
An' I never lost a copper, an' I never lost a hair.

'But I'd have lost my life the time that you've heard tell about;
I don't think I'd be settin' here, but dead beyond a doubt,
If that there Indyan "Wolverine" jest hadn't helped me out.

''Twas freshet time, 'way back, as long as sixty-six or eight,
An' I was comin' to the Post that year a kind of late,
For beaver had been plentiful, and trappin' had been great.

'One day I had been settin' traps along a bit of wood,
An' night was catchin' up to me jest faster 'an it should,
When all at once I heard a sound that curdled up my blood.

'It was the howl of famished wolves—I didn't stop to think
But jest lit out across for home as quick as you could wink,
But when I reached the river's edge I brought up at the brink.

'That mornin' I had crossed the stream straight on a sheet of ice
An' now, God help me! There it was, churned up an' cracked to
    dice,
The flood went boiling past—I stood like one shut in a vice.

'No way ahead, no path aback, trapped like a rat ashore,
With naught but death to follow, and with naught but death afore;
The howl of hungry wolves aback—ahead, the torrent's roar.

'An' then—a voice, an Indyan voice, that called out clear and clean,
"Take Indyan's horse, I run like deer, wolf can't catch Wolverine."
I says, "Thank Heaven." There stood the chief I'd nicknamed
    Wolverine.

'I leapt on that there horse, an' then jest like a coward fled,
An' left that Indyan standin' there alone, as good as dead,
With the wolves a-howlin' at his back, the swollen stream ahead.

'I don't know how them Indyans dodge from death the way they
    do,
You won't believe it, sir, but what I'm tellin' you is true,
But that there chap was 'round next day as sound as me or you.

'He came to get his horse, but not a cent he'd take from me.
Yes, sir, you're right, the Indyans now ain't like they used to be;
We've got 'em sharpened up a bit an' *now* they'll take a fee.

'No, sir, you're wrong, they ain't no "dogs". I'm not through
    tellin' yet;
You'll take that name right back again, or else jest out you get!
You'll take that name right back when you hear all this yarn, I bet.

'It happened that same autumn, when some Whites was comin' in,
I heard the old Red River carts a-kickin' up a din,
So I went over to their camp to see an English skin.

'They said, "They'd had an awful scare from Injuns", an' they
    swore
That savages had come around the very night before
A-brandishing their tomahawks an' painted up for war.

'But when their plucky Englishmen had put a bit of lead
Right through the heart of one of them, an' rolled him over, dead,
The other cowards said that they had come on peace instead.

' "That they (the Whites) had lost some stores, from off their little
    pack,
An' that the Red they peppered dead had followed up their track,
Because he'd found the packages an' came *to give them back.*"

' "Oh!" they said, "they were quite sorry, but it wasn't like as if
They had killed a decent Whiteman by mistake or in a tiff,
It was only some old Injun dog that lay there stark an' stiff."

'I said, "You are the meanest dogs that ever yet I seen,"
Then I rolled the body over as it lay out on the green;
I peered into the face—My God! 'twas poor old Wolverine.'

1912

The Train Dogs

Out of the night and the north;
   Savage of breed and of bone,
Shaggy and swift comes the yelping band,
Freighters of fur from the voiceless land
   That sleeps in the Arctic zone.

Laden with skins from the north,
   Beaver and bear and raccoon,
Marten and mink from the polar belts,
Otter and ermine and sable pelts—
   The spoils of the hunter's moon.

Out of the night and the north,
   Sinewy, fearless and fleet,
Urging the pack through the pathless snow,
The Indian driver, calling low,
   Follows with moccasined feet.

Ships of the night and the north,
   Freighters on prairies and plains,
Carrying cargoes from field and flood
They scent the trail through their wild red blood;
   The wolfish blood in their veins.

1912

ANNIE CHARLOTTE DALTON
1865–1938

The Robin's Egg

The drenched earth has a warm, sweet radiance all her own;
The wakening chestnut flings upon the air
Her crumpled loveliness of leaf.
Lovely and brief,
The daffodil stands deep
In arabis full-blown—
There, early honey gatherers come.

Gold dawns along the spare,
Sleek buds of leopard's-bane,
Beneath the autumn-planted dog-wood still asleep;
Lovely and vain,
The slim, young plum
Flaunts her white bridal veil
Beyond the garden pale.

Fallen, fallen amongst the daffodils,
A robin's egg half-crushed—
Bluer than any sky could be,
Blue with a tense divinity
As if some god had brushed,
Impatiently, a jewel from his hand—
Ah! who shall understand
This radiant mystery!

A moment, and the beauty of our garden has rushed
Away; my heart with some strange rapture fills—
This rapture of this robin's blue
Holds all my soul in thrall,
As if I heard and knew
Some strange, sweet, foreign call;

As if I saw and knew
Some secret in the robin's precious blue.

This scrap of jelly which should be,
Potentially,
A singing robin in our tree—
I sorrow for its tiny life, but still,
Intoxicating, leaps the thrill
That ravishes, that satisfies my soul,
Soothes me, and makes me whole—

So strangely are we made! If I could tell
Whence this pure rapture, this dumb spell—
So strangely are we made that I must know
Why this small thing doth move me so;
Why, for an amulet, I fain would beg
The turquoise of some robin's egg.

1910

Out of Work

There is a street down-town, where all day long,
Go silent men with lagging feet that look
As they were more familiar with rough ways
Than greasy pavements and the crowded streets;
Grey men with lagging feet and mutinous mouths—
Oh, fear those mutinous mouths, those lagging feet,
Those unseen, unraised eyes that brood and brood
On living death.

1929

The Praying-Mantis

In the dark dungeons of the mind;
Strange creatures walk and breed their kind;
 The Mantis mounts the stair,
 With movements free as air.

The Praying-Mantis mounts the stair,
Her tiny arms upheld in prayer.
 In chasuble and stole,
 She stands to read my soul.

I know not what dark thing is there,
Nor why my soul must feel despair,
 Nor why she turns away
 And bids the Mantis slay.

In the deep dungeons of the mind,
Strange creatures walk and breed their kind;
 With arms upheld in prayer
 The Mantis mounts the stair.

1935

LUCY MAUD MONTGOMERY
1874–1942

The Test

All the great house sat hushed and listening
 There 'neath the music's spell,
Laughter and tears in bright eyes were glistening
 When the painted curtain fell;
Thunderous applause uprose to greet,
 I was their darling then.
Incense and homage at my feet
 They poured, those women and men!

Think you then that my heart was flattered,
 Dream I was satisfied?
Praise or censure, it nothing mattered
 When I had glanced aside;
There in the shadows across my right
 Sat the Artist, old and grey,
Never a motion made he that night
 To approve or applaud my play!

Silent he sat when the house was cheering
 —Bitter that hour to me!

What cared I for the fickle veering
   Of fancy's wind? It was he,
He, the master, I strove to please.
   Naught had my hope availed,
That grim old veteran of victories
   Was silent . . . I had failed.

To My Enemy

Let those who will of friendship sing,
   And to its guerdon grateful be,
But I a lyric garland bring
   To crown thee, O, mine enemy!

Thanks, endless thanks, to thee I owe
   For that my lifelong journey through
Thine honest hate has done for me
   What love perchance had failed to do.

I had not scaled such weary heights
   But that I held thy scorn in fear,
And never keenest lure might match
   The subtle goading of thy sneer.

Thine anger struck from me a fire
   That purged all dull content away,
Our mortal strife to me has been
   Unflagging spur from day to day.

And thus, while all the world may laud
   The gifts of love and loyalty,
I lay my mead of gratitude
   Before thy feet, mine enemy!

1902

I Feel (Vers Libre)

I feel
Very much
Like taking
Its unholy perpetrators

By the hair
Of their heads
(If they have any hair)
And dragging them around
A few times,
And then cutting them
Into small, irregular pieces
And burying them
In the depths of the blue sea.
They are without form
And void,/ Or at least
The stuff they/ produce
Is./ They are too lazy
To hunt up rhymes;
And that
Is all
That is the matter with them.

1920

LOUISE MOREY BOWMAN
1882–1944

Moonlight and Common Day

Listen—you very very Few who will care to listen—
And I will tell you a story
Of moonlight.
Don't imagine because I try to tell stories of moonlight
That I am a poet—neurotic and mystic—
(Dearly as I love the things that some poets—neurotic and mystic—
Can write!)
As for me I love good food and beautiful clothing,
And well-ordered, punctual living
Behind tall, well-clipped hedges;
And practical, common-sense people.
But still—

Let us open my casement window, Beloved,
Where the dark leaves stir in the silence,
And the sweet, wet earth breathes softly

And murmurs an exquisite word.
Any moment out into the moonlight may issue
White creatures, and elfin-formed things that we know not,
Quaintly and solemnly marching and chaunting inaudibly.
Something stirs by the willows—
Do you know what that sound is, so lovely and shuddering?
It's the owl's cry.
The grave, small, gray owl that in purple dusk comes sometimes
To sit on my window-sill, eyes open, dreaming,—
Hark how he is linking us in with the moonlight,
Like a horn faintly blown in blue heaven.
(Do you remember, Beloved, a night,
Glad years ago in a pine-wood,
In the moon-lighted darkness—
How the rhythmical thunder of waves on the white shore
Blended with us and our heart-beats, Beloved?)

Let us lean from the window
As if faintly-blown horns have called us to answer three questions.
Is Life food and raiment and conquest?
Is Love conquest and intrigue and passion?
Is Death a gaunt figure white-shrouded
Dealing blows out of blackness?
Let us fling back our eternal 'No!' as an answer—
To the listening Silence,
While the sweet, wet earth still breathes softly
An exquisite word.

But tomorrow
I shall go right on living
As unworthy as ever of the moonlight
Locked up in my soul.

          *   *   *   *

That is my story of moonlight—
No story at all, now say you?
But it all lies written
Between the lines.

1922

Timepieces

I

There are three wise clocks in the house.
In a winter night I heard them striking twelve. . . . ,
Answering each other,
Humanly.
The tall, ancient and beautiful clock in the hall,
In an inlaid case with the Prince of Wales' feathers,
And the quaint, painted posies in the corners of the dial,
With the painted lady above the dial
Who sits on a green bank,
Holding a white cockatoo on her hand
So gracefully.
The cold, silver notes of this Clock began. . . .
And then there broke in lustily
The hoarser, more human note of the other old Grandfather's
    Clock
On the upper landing. . . .
In its plain, massive case, with the little, old ship
With wee white sails,
That rocks backward and forward. . . .
Backward. . . . forward. . . .
Charming.
The eyes of generations of small, wondering children
Climbing up to nursery tea in the twilight.
And last came the slow, ghostly striking
Of a very, very old Clock, on the library mantel. . . .
A clock who has always worked very hard
And who has to be wound every evening,
And who has never been sure of a steady, aristocratic foundation
To stand on. . . .
Like the others,
But who still strikes, feebly and truthfully,
Proud to give service.
Three old clocks very wise and human. . . .
And faithful,
Striking the hours on a winter night,
With the age-old Moon looking in at the windows.

II

In a house that is suddenly left empty,
Unlighted, alone,

Through the long mystical hours of a night
An old eightday Clock strikes. . . .
Twelve. . . .
One. . . .
Two. . . .
Three. . . .
Is there anything so silent. . . . lonely. . . . vast. . . .
As a Clock striking hours in a house. . . .
With no one to listen?
Is there no one to listen?

III
The Sundial is very, very old
To be counting the hours in my modern garden,
Where flowers bloom in wild riot of colour,
And modern poets read *vers libre*
Under the shade of a jolly young maple tree.

I think I shall plant tall, stately white phlox
All around the Sundial
Next summer.
And try to have more spaces of green, velvet turf. . . .
And perhaps buy a peacock.

For we cannot read only Elizabethan lyrics and sonnets
Beside the sundial,
And it is so aloof and so old for my modern garden,
Although, in the sunshine, so faithful. . . .
Yes, it should have a peacock!

IV
The winter moonlight is streaming down
Into the sunken garden.
Yesterday I laid a vivid spray of red Autumn berries
Upon the sundial,
Over the calm old motto. . . .
'Light and shade by turns but Love always.'

Now the first snow has fallen, and in the pale moonlight
The Sundial stands as aloof as ever on its slender pedestal. . . .
Holding quietly a white crown,
Dropped lightly upon it
From the mysterious sky that holds the Sun and the Moon.

v
I have written these sketches of clocks and a sundial
Waiting in the power-house of a great factory. . . .
Where a chair is courteously placed for me
In a bare, lofty room
Between two monstrous whirring engines
Apparently ceaseless.
At first their rush and their crashing roar
Terrified me.
I wanted to scream and to run. . . . gasping. . . .
Now the noise has become rhythmical. . . . awesome. . . .
And I think, queerly, of deep, green caverns
Far under the roar of the ocean.
How slow. . . . slow. . . . slow
The old clocks striking at midnight. . . .

In comparison
With this hurrying, rhythmical beat of these mighty engines,
Timed to the fraction of a second.
High over my head, on a brick wall
A shrill piercing gong strikes now and then rapidly. . . .
Cleaving the roar and the rhythm. . . .
I understand nothing. . . .

* * * * * * * * * * *

Now I shall simply write down, laboriously. . . .
As a child writes. . . .
And very reverently. . . .
GOD
SUNDIALS
CLOCKS
ENGINES
TIME AND ETERNITY.

1922

Sea Lavender

My Puritan Grandmother!—I see her now,
With placid brow,
Always so sure
'That no things but the right things shall endure!'
Sombrely neat, so orderly and prim,

Always a little grim,
Austere but kind. . . .
Smooth-banded hair and smoothly-banded mind.

But let me whisper it to you today—
I know it now—
That deep in her there was a flame at play.
Beneath that brow
The blue-grey eyes sought beauty, found it too
Most often by the ocean's passionate blue.
Her sea-beach treasures—shells and coloured weed
Gathered and hoarded with glad human greed—
They warm my heart today with insight new.
How vividly I see her, frail and old,
A tiny, black-clothed figure on the beach,
Compactly wrapped against the sea-wind's cold,
Patiently waiting till waves let her reach
Some sandy strip, where purple, amber, green,
Her lacy sea-weed treasures could be seen.
(She pressed and mounted them—frail tangled things!
Handled by her, fit to trim fairies' wings.)

So I recall her,
Searching salt-sea pools
For Beauty's shadow.
All her rigid rules,
And cold austereness with a storm-tossed child,
Melt into airs of evenings, warm and mild.
And I find revelation, sweet indeed
In her dear treasures of sea shells and weed.

1922

MARJORIE PICKTHALL
1883–1922

Père Lalement

I lift the Lord on high,
Under the murmuring hemlock boughs, and see
The small birds of the forest lingering by
And making melody.
These are mine acolytes and these my choir,

And this mine altar in the cool green shade,
Where the wild soft-eyed does draw nigh
Wondering, as in the byre
Of Bethlehem the oxen heard Thy cry
And saw Thee, unafraid.

My boatmen sit apart,
Wolf-eyed, wolf-sinewed, stiller than the trees.
Help me, O Lord, for very slow of heart
And hard of faith are these.
Cruel are they, yet Thy children. Foul are they,
Yet wert Thou born to save them utterly.
Then make me as I pray
Just to their hates, kind to their sorrows, wise
After their speech, and strong before their free
Indomitable eyes.

Do the French lilies reign
Over Mount Royal and Stadacona still?
Up the St Lawrence comes the spring again,
Crowning each southward hill
And blossoming pool with beauty, while I roam
Far from the perilous folds that are my home,
There where we built St Ignace for our needs,
Shaped the rough roof tree, turned the first sweet sod,
St Ignace and St Louis, little beads
On the rosary of God.

Pines shall Thy pillars be,
Fairer than those Sidonian cedars brought
By Hiram out of Tyre, and each birch-tree
Shines like a holy thought.
But come no worshippers; shall I confess,
St Francis-like, the birds of the wilderness?
O, with Thy love my lonely head uphold.
A wandering shepherd I, who hath no sleep;
A wandering soul, who hath no scrip, nor gold,
Nor anywhere to sleep.

My hour of rest is done;
On the smooth ripple lifts the long canoe;
The hemlocks murmur sadly as the sun
Slants his dim arrows through.

Whither I go I know not, nor the way,
Dark with strange passions, vexed with heathen charms,
Holding I know not what of life or death;
Only be Thou beside me day by day,
Thy rod my guide and comfort, underneath
Thy everlasting arms.

1913

The Little Sister of the Prophet

'If there arise among you a prophet or dreamer . . .'

I have left a basket of dates
In the cool dark room that is under the vine,
Some curds set out in two little crimson plates
And a flask of the amber wine,
And cakes most cunningly beaten
Of savoury herbs, and spice, and the delicate wheaten
Flour that is best,
And all to lighten his spirit and sweeten his rest.

This morning he cried, 'Awake,
And see what the wonderful grace of the Lord hath revealed!'
And we ran for his sake,
But 'twas only the dawn outspread o'er our father's field,
And the house of the potter white in the valley below.
But his hands were upraised to the east and he cried to us, 'So
Ye may ponder and read
The strength and the beauty of God outrolled in a fiery screed!'

Then the little brown mother smiled,
As one does on the words of a well-loved child,
And, 'Son,' she replied, 'have the oxen been watered and fed?
For work is to do, though the skies be never so red,
And already the first sweet hours of the day are spent.'
And he sighed and went.

Will he come from the byre
With his head all misty with dreams, and his eyes on fire,
Shaking us all with the weight of the words of his passion?
I will give him raisins instead of dates,
And wreathe young leaves on the little red plates.
I will put on my new head-tyre,

And braid my hair in a comelier fashion.
Will he note? Will he mind?
Will he touch my cheek as he used to, and laugh and be kind?

1913

Ebb Tide

The Sailor's Grave at Clo-oose, V.I.

Out of the winds' and the waves' riot,
Out of the loud foam,
He has put in to a great quiet
And a still home.

Here he may lie at ease and wonder
Why the old ship waits,
And hark for the surge and the strong thunder
Of the full Straits,

And look for the fishing fleet at morning,
Shadows like lost souls,
Slide through the fog where the seal's warning
Betrays the shoals,

And watch for the deep-sea liner climbing
Out of the bright West,
With a salmon-sky and her wake shining
Like a tern's breast,—

And never know he is done for ever
With the old sea's pride,
Borne from the fight and the full endeavour
On an ebb tide.

1922

Quiet

Come not the earliest petal here, but only
Wind, cloud, and star,
Lovely and far,
Make it less lonely.

Few are the feet that seek her here, but sleeping
Thoughts sweet as flowers
Linger for hours,
Things winged, yet weeping.

Here in the immortal empire of the grasses,
Time, like one wrong
Note in a song,
With their bloom, passes.

1922

The Wife

Living, I had no might
To make you hear,
Now, in the inmost night,
I am so near
No whisper, falling light,
Divides us, dear.

Living, I had no claim
On your great hours.
Now the thin candle-flame,
The closing flowers,
Wed summer with my name,—
And these are ours.

Your shadow on the dust,
Strength, and a cry,
Delight, despair, mistrust,—
All these am I.
Dawn, and the far hills thrust
To a far sky.

Living, I had no skill
To stay your tread,
Now all that was my will
Silence has said.
We are one for good and ill
Since I am dead.

1922

KATHERINE HALE
(Amelia Beers Garvin)
1887–1956

Grey Knitting

All through the country, in the autumn stillness,
  A web of grey spreads strangely, rim to rim;
And you may hear the sound of knitting needles,
  Incessant, gentle,—dim.

A tiny click of little wooden needles,
  Elfin amid the gianthood of war;
Whispers of women, tireless and patient,
  Who weave the web afar.

Whispers of women, tireless and patient—
  'Foolish, inadequate!' we hear you say;
'Grey wool on fields of hell is out of fashion,'
  And yet we weave the web from day to day.

Suppose some soldier dying, gaily dying;
  Under the alien skies, in his last hour,
Should listen, in death's prescience so vivid,
  And hear a fairy sound bloom like a flower—

I like to think that soldiers, gaily dying
  For the white Christ on fields with shame sown deep,
May hear the fairy click of women's needles,
  As they fall fast asleep.

1914

At Eighty

One sees her brougham still,
As she goes calling with her silver case,
Something about her like a rare old lace
Woven of metallic thread.

She recalls candlelight,
Harpstrings, and backgrounds of a rich brocade

Where Dresden figures, delicate yet staid,
Were wont to dance.

Ghosts are her only partners,
Rakish young gentlemen of years ago,
Whose solemn looks and wigs of powdered snow
Belie their wordly ways.

It is precise music;
A little arrogant, and sweet and thin,
It does not let one wailing measure in—
Not even the last bar!

1934

Fourth Dimensional

This flimsy tent
On the dark forest's edge
Faces such cold blue water
And length of russet sedge.

Open to night,
A tree holds out the rain
Or melts to wavering shadow
Upon our roof again.

Within the tent
Lord God for you and me!
From violent root to blossoming flower
The whole ecstatic tree.

Oh, as we lay
Deep in the stillness there,
Knowing that we should sink
Out of all mortal air

Down into that sweet death,
I quite believed, you know,
That a Fourth Door might open,

Or a torn fold would show
Trace of the long-lost passage—
And yet, it was not so! . . .

1934

MARTHA OSTENSO
1900–1963

A Far Land

Dark cannot blot the dark
In the place I know,
Rain cannot drown the rain,
Wind cannot blow
The wind of that stormed land,
Where stillness falls
On sudden wings, like a band
Of quiet birds on ruined walls.

1924

The Return

Oh, strong and faithful and enduring
As my mother's face,
The sowing of the years has wrought
No change in you, no ill,
Wild field that I loved! The generous grace ·
Of ragweed and of nettle caught
In the ruddy fall of sun
And in the silvering of rain enveils you still,
And here and there a warm rut of the dun
And patient earth with small, slow life is stirring.

Your stiff, pale grass and weedy flowers
Still proudly grow
Innocent of being beautiless—
(Even a little vain,
Trusting no leafed thing could be low
That the sky-born rain would bless)
And oh! the sunny smell of you—

Of brittling stems, sweet spears long-matted lain
In spider weft and gold-pricked dust and dew
Through the dream and languidness of humming hours.

Under the blackbird swartly flying
From west to east,
Under the reach of the lark from north to south
You are my field—the same
Brown curve along the sky—even the least
Brown blade the same. To lay my mouth
On the quiet of your dew-sweet face
And hear the deep earth of you call my name—
This is to know that I have found my place—
And the empty years have ended all their crying.

1924

Caution

Let us go dressed in wind
That only the piquant buds of the white birch tree
May see us.

Let us go dressed in rain
That only the sad ghost swaying in the willow tree
May see us.

Let us not garland
The shining, naked bodies of one another,
Lest in the scattered silver of the moon
The white tulip tree blossom green with bitterness.

1924

AUDREY ALEXANDRA BROWN
b. 1904

Candles in the Glass

Here in this ivory room whose pale casket
Holds bright-gowned women like bright fruit heaped
     in a basket,
A man at the piano strikes out chords

Of a crashing march; silent we sit and listen
To the great notes that glisten, wheel and glisten
With the hard brilliance of the play of swords.

Silent we sit and listen, each in our places;
Yet I am aware behind the stilled faces
Of a restless hovering like the wings of birds—
Of small inconsequent currents of thought leaping
From mind to mind, never silenced or sleeping
Or able to appease themselves in words.

There is a mirror on the wall nearest:
I need not lift my eyes to see this clearest
Of clear lovely things, in which I have found
A lovelier, whose beauty makes me ache with yearning—
Three tall reflected candles quietly burning
Without flicker of flame in that bright round.

The currents of thought dart under—over—under—
The music mounts till it shakes the air with its thunder:
And all the while unmoved in that clear plane
Is the delicate fire of the three candles burning,
Like that serene far Light towards which our yearning
Beats up from the dark forever, sick to attain.

1937

The Whistler

I remember a boy,
   Sauntering, his hands in his pockets, down the street,
   And whistling loud and sweet
For very joy.

It was in a morning of May:
   I, a child, heard note on clear note
   Tumbled headlong from a human throat;
I looked out, I saw him going his way

Idly and gladly with unpurposed foot
   Between the white and purple lilac trees—
   Piping his heart's ease
On his live flute.

Why have I not forgotten boy and bough?
  On some unlike day, I pause—
  I remember; I wonder who and what he was,
And if he's as happy now.

1943

The Island

Eastward lies the Island,
In a bay of raw sapphire streaked with shoals;
The tide rolls,
Beating itself to pieces in the jaws
Of broken-fanged reefs as white as bone;
Spray splinters on stone
Of the sharply-rising waterless soil-less highland—
Such is the Island.

There no man lives nor may, but there each year
The seals heavily
Drag themselves up the smooth rock from the sea—
Their soft eyes confident, their hides sleek—
Coming without haste, without fear,
To the citadel they seek.
Here, these unbefriending wastes among,
Yearly are born their young:
Here and thus
Yearly however temporarily,
The solitude is populous
With the stupid gentle people of the sea.

Along the road that rounds the bay is a slope;
Half-way down the slope to the sea is a house—
Built so cunningly into the slope-stair,
Screened so darkly by fir and the fir boughs,
You might pass and pass and never know it was there.
In that house there lives a lady
Whose glassed wall looks steadfastly
Down the wild fall of rock to the sea
And the roaring reef and the spume flying
And ever and evermore
About the shore
The gulls crying, the gulls wheeling and crying.

I have seen her once: she was strange and beautiful—tall,
With milk-white hair and a dead-white face; she went
Sumptuous in green brocade and golden roses:
I looked, I was not content
To look and pass; my heart said, 'Winter closes;
What will you do, O lady, when outside
Is only the far country white and wide
And the listening firs at the door, and ceaselessly
The cannonading sea?'

What will you do, O lady? Night and day
The sound of the mad surf that never lulls
Is in your heart, and the cry of the mad gulls.
Do they say true, the gossips, when they say
Whisperingly,
*That a white seal haunts the Island
When the grey seals come up from the sea?*

1943

FLORIS CLARKE McLAREN
b. 1904

Bits of the Pattern

There were things she remembered as she grew,
Small bright bits of the pattern of things she knew:

    There was always the Valley,
    Always a strong wind blowing,
    And the bay, and the mountains,
    So that she grew up knowing
    Stars and their changes,
    White windflowers in spring;
    And that darkness could be
    A safe and friendly thing.

Sometimes in winter, when the north wind tore
Down through the rocky funnel of the hills,
Her father met her at the schoolhouse door.
The tears froze on her face before they fell,
But seeing him there she was suddenly unafraid
Of the stinging snow and the bitter howling day;

And stepping carefully behind his steps
She found the only shelter on the way,
The small safe haven that his broad back made.

Through spring and summer she watched the brush piled high
In the south clearing, seasoned, tinder-dry;
Till one rain-threatened afternoon in fall,
Just at first dusk, she heard her father call,
And running close beside him where the trees
Had taken strangeness with the night, she reached
The clearing; watched him bend to light
A tiny flame that wavered, kindled, spread,
Till orange banners leaped above her head
And swarming sparks whirled bright against the sky.
So she learned the wonder of flame and spark,
Of sudden roaring beauty in the dark.

Sharper than other terrors was the ford:
The pitch and jolting as the horses stepped
Into the current, and the rising swirl
Of cold green water pulling at the wheels,
Foaming hub-deep to splash the wagon floor;
The sickening roll of glacier-polished stones
And that eternity in full mid-stream,
Always the same, that moment when it seemed
She moved and not the water; strangely swept
With sure and dreadful swiftness up the tide.
That was the worst. Too terrified to cry
She clutched the wagon edge until they came
To splashing shallows, and the horses strained
In a last plunging scramble up the bank
To sun-warmed willows on the other side.

All through her life the smell of dawn could bring
A sudden choking memory of the way
The great bulk of East Mountain rode the sky,
With sun behind it, and the morning haze
Thin-drifting; overshadowing her days
So that she never quite forgot how small
The town, the people, looked beneath that wall.

Clouds and their shadows; always the keen wind blowing;
The grey light of spring evenings, water flowing;

These were things she remembered as she grew,
Clear bright bits of the pattern of things she knew.

1937

South Flight

Low grey sky and a pattern of wild geese flying,
And you'll stop with twisted heart to watch their flight;
Still standing, after the long wedge streams from sight.
Straining your ears for the last thin sound of their crying.

There'll be snow by morning, and cold wind-fingers prying
At chink and crevice, so fasten the windows tight.
And bring fresh wood for the fire, but in the night
You'll wake with a sob, remembering that distant crying,
Low grey sky and a pattern of wild geese flying.

1937

DOROTHY ROBERTS
b. 1906

Cold

My grandparents lived to a great age in the cold—
O cruel preservative, the hard day beginning
With night and zero and the firewood
Numbing the fingers. God could have been in the flame
Responsive among the birch sticks, roaring
Up through the comforting pipes, and served all day
From the frosted woodpile, the continuing flame
As the sun almost let go of the bitter world.

But for them He stayed in the cold,
In the outer absolutes of cold among the fiery orbits,
And gave them the white breath and the blood pumping
Through hard activity stringing out the muscles
Into great age. They lived in cold
And were seasoned by it and preached it
And knew that it blazed

In the burning bush of antiquity
With starry flowers.

1957

Old Japanese Prints

Distance is measured by feet to another village,
The trail goes over ice, the click of feet
Goes all through the centuries. Civilization sits
Even on a volcano and will not move.

The waves have talons, the faces are flecks of foam,
The faces have nothing to fear in the thin boats,
The faces are not; that is the secret of living
Here in the settled snow where the bamboo shivers.

Ceremonious as a firecracker the habitual cone
Centres the picture, the great pine invites the rain,
The figures follow the centuries in a simple order,
There are changes enough from within when the trees flower.

1961

The Farm

My father was taken with the land
And after a long war
Came to it with a weather eye for bounty,
Praised what grew.

Trilliums, the painted and the simple,
Mushrooms round among the rainy crows,
And even the hard pebbles of the river
He cultivated like the knotted apple.

Following his quest within the living cycle
He served the ends of things in field and burrow
And quiet climb of spruce beyond the pasture.

Horses cost most to carry, traded down to
The weathered old one that his pity knew

And wouldn't sell for fear she'd turn to glue
And so miss out on heaven—

Heaven came true
Only when reached through earth. Soft-sounding rain
Raised the brooks loudly till the golden drought
Ran in the flood and with the striking cold

Brought benefits low, prized fragrances and texture
Downed to the root or stalk (but rose thereafter
And were as pink as ever in neglected pasture).

Prepared for the great blow, he raised a special
Expanse of radiance over the cold hill
Where gallop about in my diviner eye
The broken horses with their bits of gold.

1961

Veranda Spinsters

If they are gone—and they must be gone—
The audience, and so the drama, is less.
Hot afternoon, elm-arched, brought their ensconcing
Of selves along the porch in odd best dress.

Eyes in a row veering to east, to west
Soon caught our coming with a stir of pleasure
Communicated to us till we stepped
More brightly into their expectant leisure.

In setting of shade and sunlight and old houses
We felt ourselves encompassed in a meaning
Beyond our presence—we were young, they seasoned
With summers and summers of this absorbent leaning.

Their thoughts expanding us, we bowed, they bowed
And their three spreading smiles grew vast, became
Applause which, remembered, fixes us again,
Focused in sunlight, into the town's frame.

1961

Provider

On the stem of the father the daughter: he took me at zero
To the farm he was thinking of buying far off in the wilds,
There in the frozen north it stood a weird world
Of itself with lambs in the kitchen behind the hot stove—
And there he was placed in position to be his own Word.

On the hill with the hollows surrounding and forests strewn wide
Stood the house, stood the barn, ploughed the footsteps
                                    through the white tide
Of snow decreasing, increasing under sun and high cold,
And into those elements melted my father of the world
And formed again hardened and extended in rein, plough
and sward.

By the footsteps in snow counted deeply, in wind smothered over
Was caught the frame house to the barn, back and forth
                                    morning and evening
By lantern, by cold, by conditions, quiet and eerie
Attaching the beasts to our hopes in their sun-chinked eternity—
Over the distance our passing more than back and forth only.

And out to the forest for wood that would waken our chimney
Billowing into the blue, we were gone. There were only
The fence tops between us and forests of dark melancholy,
But wind had made distance gigantic. We crossed it and followed
The faint road on into the depths where our white logs were piled.

Come, high stars, and find me as solemn as there in the forest,
My friends the white tracks in the snow, and find me as open
To anything coming or going, and grow me as welcome
There on the bough of all being in the great semicircle,
Come, winter, and grow me again where my father once
                                    brought me.

1967

Winter

Woods deeply withdrawn part company with us
who must go on to real death—

for which we seek some other analogy parallel to us
as the autumn images have seemed to be.

This doesn't go far enough but becomes winter
cold in the full blast and the shapes contorted
and the solstice turning the year around again
no matter how diligent it may seem to be.

Woods deeply withdrawn hold glittering streams of iridescence
from the sun when the ice sheathes
the twigs in their scintillating ringing like bells
it is winter, the depth, and the year turns.

This doesn't go far enough but for the forms
blocked in the ice, the snow, the cold that stays
as the year travels on holding in its perspective
the distant and stirring spring with its own purpose.

The cold settles in arrested where the wind whittled
the landscape into the forms of strange wisdom
holding there the analogy, holding it rigid
under the cold sparkle and the iridescence.

1976

DOROTHY LIVESAY
b. 1909

Green Rain

I remember long veils of green rain
Feathered like the shawl of my grandmother—
Green from the half-green of the spring trees
Waving in the valley.

I remember the road
Like the one which leads to my grandmother's house,
A warm house, with green carpets,
Geraniums, a trilling canary
And shining horse-hair chairs;
And the silence, full of the rain's falling
Was like my grandmother's parlour

Alive with herself and her voice, rising and falling—
Rain and wind intermingled.

I remember on that day
I was thinking only of my love
And of my love's house.
But now I remember the day
As I remember my grandmother.
I remember the rain as the feathery fringe of her shawl.

1932

The Three Emilys*

These women crying in my head
Walk alone, uncomforted:
The Emilys, these three
Cry to be set free—
And others whom I will not name
Each different, each the same.

Yet they had liberty!
Their kingdom was the sky:
They batted clouds with easy hand,
Found a mountain for their stand;
From wandering lonely they could catch
The inner magic of a heath—
A lake their palette, any tree
Their brush could be.

And still they cry to me
As in reproach—
I, born to hear their inner storm
Of separate man in woman's form,
I yet possess another kingdom, barred
To them, these three, this Emily.
I move as mother in a frame,
My arteries
Flow the immemorial way
Towards the child, the man;
And only for brief span

*Emily Brontë, Emily Dickinson, and Emily Carr.

Am I an Emily on mountain snows
And one of these.

And so the whole that I possess
Is still much less—
They move triumphant through my head:
I am the one
Uncomforted.

1953

Bartok and the Geranium

She lifts her green umbrellas
Towards the pane
Seeking her fill of sunlight
Or of rain;
Whatever falls
She has no commentary
Accepts, extends,
Blows out her furbelows,
Her bustling boughs;

And all the while he whirls
Explodes in space,
Never content with this small room:
Not even can he be
Confined to sky
But must speed high and higher still
From galaxy to galaxy,
Wrench from the stars their momentary notes
Steal music from the moon.

She's daylight
He is dark
She's heaven-held breath
He storms and crackles
Spits with hell's own spark.

Yet in this room, this moment now
These together breathe and be:
She, essence of serenity,
He in a mad intensity

Soars beyond sight
From heaven's height.

And when he's done, he's out:
She leans a lip against the glass
And preens herself in light.

1955

Without Benefit of Tape

The real poems are being written in outports
on backwoods farms
in passageways where pantries still exist
or where geraniums
nail light to the window
while out of the window boy in the flying field
is pulled to heaven on the keel of a kite.

Stories breed in the north:
men with snow in their mouths
trample and shake at the bit
kneading the woman down under blankets of snow
icing her breath, her eyes.

The living speech is shouted out
by men and women leaving railway lines
to trundle home, pack-sacked
just company for deer or bear—

    Hallooed
across the counter, in a corner store
it booms upon the river's shore:
on midnight roads where hikers flag you down
speech echoes from the canyon's wall
    resonant
    indubitable.

1967

The Uninvited

Always a third one's there
where any two are walking out
along a river-bank   so mirror-still
sheathed in sheets
of sky   pillows of cloud—
their footprints crunch the hardening earth
their eyes delight in trees   stripped clean
winter-prepared
with only the rose-hips red
and the plump fingers of sumach

And always between the two
(scuffling the leaves, laughing
and fingers locked)
goes a third lover   his or hers
who walked this way with one or other   once
flung back the head   snapped branches of dark pine
in armfuls   before snowfall

      I walk beside you
      trace
      a shadow's shade
      skating on silver
      hear
      another voice
      singing under ice

1971

The Artefacts: West Coast

In the middle of the night
I hear this old house breathing
a steady sigh
when oak trees and rock shadows
assemble silence
under a high
white moon

I hear the old house turn
in its sleep

shifting the weight of long dead footsteps
from one wall to another
echoing the children's voices
shrilly calling
from one room to the next
repeating those whispers in the master bedroom
a cry, a long sigh of breath
from one body to another
when the holy ghost takes over

In the middle of the night
I wake
and hear time speaking

First it was forest; rock;
hidden ups and downs
a hill where oaks and pines
struggled
and if a stranger climbed
the topmost pine
he'd see the ocean flattening the mountains
the forest, serried—
below, only the sculpted bays
native encampments
ceremonial lodges, totem poles
and winter dances
the Raven overall
giver-of-light, supervising
and the white whale imminent
evil lurking
to be appeased with ritual
long hair dancing
fathered masks

    But history begins
the woman said
    when you are thirty
    that tomtom, time
    begins to beat
    to beat for you

And in this city on the brink
of forest—sea—

history delights that Queen Victoria
made marriage with the totem wilderness
the cedar silences
the raven's wing

Now ravens build here still
Seagulls spiral
the happy children in these attics
breathe and cry
unwittingly
the names of history
tumble from their lips:
Nootka   Nanaimo
Maset   Ucluelet
The map leaps up

> *here did I live*
> *was born and reared*
> *here died*

So also said Chief Maquinna   Jewitt   Emily Carr

The map leaps up
from namelessness
to history
each place made ceremonial
when named
and its name
peopled!
events shouted!

> *here the waters divided*
> *here the whale bellowed*

In the middle of the night
the house heaves, unmoored
launched on a vast sea.

1971

ANNE WILKINSON
1910–1961

Lens

I
The poet's daily chore
Is my long duty;
To keep and cherish my good lens
For love and war
And wasps about the lilies
And mutiny within.

My woman's eye is weak
And veiled with milk;
My working eye is muscled
With a curious tension,
Stretched and open
As the eyes of children;
Trusting in its vision
Even should it see
The holy holy spirit gambol
Counterheadwise,
Lithe and warm as any animal.

My woman's iris circles
A blind pupil;
The poet's eye is crystal,
Polished to accept the negative,
The contradictions in a proof
And the accidental
Candour of the shadows;

The shutter, oiled and smooth
Clicks on the grace of heroes
Or on some bestial act
When lit with radiance
The afterwords the actors speak
Give depths to violence,

Or if the bull is great
And the matador
And the sword
Itself the metaphor.

II
In my dark room the years
Lie in solution,
Develop film by film.
Slow at first and dim
Their shadows bite
On the fine white pulp of paper.

An early snap of fire
Licking the arms of air
I hold against the light, compare
The details with a prehistoric view
Of land and sea
And cradles of mud that rocked
The wet and sloth of infancy.

A stripe of tiger, curled
And sleeping on the ribs of reason
Prints as clear
As Eve and Adam, pearled
With sweat, staring at an apple core;

And death, in black and white
Or politic in green and Easter film,
Lands on steely points, a dancer
Disciplined to the foolscap stage,
The property of poets
Who command his robes, expose
His moving likeness on the page.

1955

Carol

I was a lover of turkey and holly
But my true love was the Christmas tree
We hung our hearts from a green green bough
And merry swung the mistletoe

We decked the tree with a silver apple
And a golden pear,
A partridge and a cockle shell
And a fair maiden

No rose can tell the fumes of myrrh
That filled the forest of our day
Till fruit and shell and maid fell down
And the partridge flew away

Now I swing from a brittle twig
For the green bough of my true love hid
A laily worm. Around my neck
The hangman ties the holly.

1955

In June and Gentle Oven

In June and gentle oven
Summer kingdoms simmer
As they come
And flower and leaf and love
Release
Their sweetest juice.

No wind at all
On the wide green world
Where fields go stroll-
ing by
And in and out
An adder of a stream
Parts the daisies
On a small Ontario farm.

And where, in curve of meadow,
Lovers, touching, lie,
A church of grass stands up
And walls them, holy, in.

Fabulous the insects
Stud the air
Or walk on running water,
Klee-drawn saints
And bright as angels are.

Honeysuckle here
Is more than bees can bear

And time turns pale
And stops to catch its breath
And lovers slip their flesh
And light as pollen
Play on treble water
Till bodies reappear
And a shower of sun
To dry their languor.

Then two in one the lovers lie
And peel the skin of summer
With their teeth
And suck its marrow from a kiss
So charged with grace
The tongue, all knowing
Holds the sap of June
Aloof from seasons, flowing.

1955

Daily the Drum

'If we had a keen vision and feeling . . .
it would be like hearing the grass grow
or the squirrel's heart beat,
and we should die of that roar
which lies on the other side of silence.'
                    —GEORGE ELIOT

I
Daily the drum is burst
It is not only or foremost
The din of squirrel hearts
Or the spangled noise of grass
These are simple sounds
Like bird love,
Not the sounds we die of.

II
On the other side of silence
I can hear the bones
Of bold and trembling girls

Clacking castanets
In dance of fire and fear

And who is deaf enough
When young men cry
And hailstones break the panes
That glaze the lovers' eye,
Or terror's tin scream rises,
Not from a throat
But from the key that locks
The sickness in the mouth?

The service at our graves
Comes clear, and bells,
But who can bear
The hidden grinding mirth
When etiquette conceals
The date and nature of our death?

And every hour a child's
Black coal of trouble
Picks at the poet's ear
Sharper than any other,
For child and poet wind
A one-day clock. 'NOW,'
It strikes, 'NOW is forever.'

These are the sounds that murder.

1955

KAY SMITH
b. 1911

The One Stem

In the green and silver chorus of the grass
they lose themselves, the bright particulars.

Discovery begins
in the single that is singular,
the one stem your eyes are suddenly unsealed to see,
jointed with the latest, fragile, golden light.

Go hand in hand with generalities,
you will never be surprised,
you will never cross over

to the child dancing to herself
in a swirl of sunlight in the blind street,
to the travelling star in the running stream,
or the lucky clover.

You will never reach that tall one
talking with clouds as he mends a roof,
or the naiad rising from birth of waters in the stone
                                                    fountain,
or under birds crossing the air, your voice will never
                                                    carry
to the old saint sweeping leaves and frost jewels in
                              the autumn morning.

1978

The Skeleton in the Closet

The skeleton was in the closet
she hung it there after the ravens
had picked it clean
she asked herself
              What could be neater
              for my narrow closet
              what could be cleaner
              than bones stripped bare
The skeleton was in the closet
and she was in the kitchen
she hummed and stirred the porridge
with a wooden spoon
              What could be safer
              than a skeleton in a closet
              all but forgotten behind the door
              what could be tamer
              than a skull with empty sockets
              what less accusing
              than a skull without a tongue
              what could be safer
              than a skeleton in a closet
              for one whose secret pocket hides the key

From time to time the season winter
she unlocked the door
when nothing but the moon
peeked in her window
and every time the bones looked whiter
than the time before
but afterwards she always locked the door
        As the clock ticked away
        and the calendar months shrivelled
        she visited less often
        her prisoner in the closet
        though sometimes she fingered
        lovingly the key

One day looking up
from the garment she was patching
she saw surprised that winter had ended
the world was a lamb frisking in a green meadow
and a tree was opening shiny leaves
like a girl's mouth for kisses
        That night upon her narrow bed
        she dreamed of openings
        those of petals virgins envelopes
        containing lovers' letters tombs
        cocoons windows doors wombs
        and children's round luminous eyes
        floating on thin stalks in darkness
        over and around the narrow bed
        where she was lying
Suddenly the dream shattered
the closet door was opening
how could it a locked door
the key hidden in her secret pocket
        But the senses took what the mind rejected
        she could feel its breath hear breathing
        Its breathing? His? Some passing stranger's?
        God present? the Devil perhaps?
Whoever or whatever
full length she felt a weight upon her
hands burned up the gown of frost
covering her from neck to ankle
then reached the flesh then something

that was not the flesh
not even the bright moon could classify
nor she could name
but she felt it like her heart
as it ascended on strong and steady wings
the steep abyss where she was falling
and JUBILATE sang a voice and it was hers
              When morning came she woke
              to see the imprint of a head
              beside hers on the pillow

              and all the windows and the doors
              except the skeleton's
              were open to a silence deeper
              than the silence of the snow that
              once had wound cold arms around her
Trembling she rose
and in her nakedness and terror
tried to open that closed door
but it was locked
and when she somehow found the strength
to find the key where it had lain a lifetime
in her secret pocket and the strength to put
the key where it belonged
              the door swung wide
              and hanging staring at her
              from within the closet
                    nothing

And JUBILATE sang the sun through all her windows
And JUBILATE sang the bird outside her door
And JUBILATE sang the wound between her thighs

1978

Old Women and Love

Drowning
no end to it

Yeats should have discovered Byzantium
as no country for old women

yet they refuse to die
they clutter up the earth
the blood of old women continues to cry out
to sing even to dance wildly in their veins
Sometimes the blood of an old woman rustles
like a starled bird when love's stealthy step
cracks the dry undergrowth in the frosty air
as if a firecracker were exploding

It seems that love is a hunter of undiscriminating taste
Women old enough to know better—though God is never
    old enough—
dream deeper and deeper into the wood
like the misty-eyed girls they once were
Suddenly one will stop astounded as the trap
love has set closes its steel jaws on a foot of frail bones

This morning very early in this silent house of sleepers
when my eyes opened from the mercy of my own darkness
the world came at me like a blow
Its beauty burned gold in every resurrected leaf
burned with a still flame   Spring never relents
What was I doing here?   What *was* I doing here?
Behind the house the trees slept paired in their cool shadows

At night an old woman on her narrow bed
probing the dark with a stubborn mind
demanding answers she knows she will not find
tends with a fierce joy the unextinguished embers
of a not so temperate love

1987

ANNE MARRIOTT
b. 1913

Prairie Graveyard

Wind mutters thinly on the sagging wire
binding the graveyard from the gouged dirt road,
bends thick-bristled Russian thistle,
sifts listless dust

into cracks in hard grey ground.
Empty prairie slides away
on all sides, rushes toward a wide
expressionless horizon, joined
to a vast blank sky.

> Lots near the road are the most expensive
> where heavy tombstones lurch a fraction
> tipped by splitting soil.
> Farther, a row of nameless heaps
> names weatherworn from tumbled sticks
> remember now the six thin children
> of a thin, shiftless home.

Hawk, wind-scouring, cuts
a pointed shadow in the drab scant grass.

> Two graves apart by the far fence
> are suicides, one with a grand
> defiant tombstone, bruising at the heart
> 'Death is swallowed up in victory'.
> (And may be, God's kindness being more large
> than man's, to this, who after seven years
> of drought, burned down his barn,
> himself hanged in it.)
> The second, nameless, set around
> with even care-sought stones
> (no stones on this section)
> topped with two plants, hard-dried,
> in rust-thick jam-tins set in the caked pile.

A gopher jumps from a round cave,
sprints furtively, spurts under fence, is gone.
Wind raises dead curls of dust, and whines
under its harsh breath on the limp dragged wires,
then leaves the graveyard stiff with silence, lone
in the centre of the huge lone land and sky.

1940

Port Renfrew

The first time I heard it *Renfrew* in our kitchen
Miss Quick who cleaned on Tuesdays
married a lighthouse keeper
('Going to do light housekeeping!'
my mother, kind, laughed every time).
Coast names hung over the linoleum
with the dust from her sweeping
Pachena Point Bamfield Tofino
I saw them green and white
like the oilcloth wallpaper
the kitchen grew windy
the walls swirled and eddied
noisy with waves.

Later he and I started out once when the children were little
a crying day though it hadn't rained all August
the raw road hot with cedar
but tears and flies and the breaking bridge
over the baked gully
ended the expedition.

Now I come alone
(if bridges collapse
at this time of life
it's too bad but not tragic)
through the stony afternoon
by the signs proceed at your own risk
thinking how often
I have tried to reach oceans
but this time there are no road blocks
the San Juan river
rolls off the map under the bridge
I check the village
then back to the beach
charting the coast curve the rock
off the south point
the bent firs the alders
the gulls and osprey wheeling.

Sitting on the silky log
I remember for no reason
a friend saying

'my husband is not my soulmate'
I have neither mate nor soulmate
(I have seen a soulmate
he did not see me)

Gulls wheel
osprey levels
ocean irresistible pushes in past
Cape Flattery
ignores borders boundaries
breaks on this beach.
The osprey swoops
the gulls settle
the waves are breaking
I have neither mate nor soulmate
but I have reached an ocean.

I caress the glass mouth of a clamshell
polished by a thousand ebbings and flowings
my friend said also 'now
is all you are certain of now'.
I am certain of all this
I write it down and keep it for certain
the osprey the gulls the alders running
the ocean wind roaring softly under the sky
and the surf breaking over over
and over
on the coarse grey changing
unchanging Port Renfrew sand.

1978

From *Letters From Some Islands*

JULY 25

Report on sightseeing:
the golden spruce
sun-caught
glowing metal
spearing its duller neighbours.
Only one in the world
(although I've heard

rumours to the contrary)
in any case unable to reproduce.
Monarch of the forest
majestic
magnificent
misfit—
how much better to be one
of two of a kind.

1985

Story from Utah

The word of the Lord
they say here
rose out of the ground.
But this was a devil
rising beside her
in his hand
the incredible gun.

Her ten-speed skidded as he sprang
fell wheels spinning as she fought
then hope   a car
on the dazzling highway   .
but the woman inside terrified
looking out
stepped on the gas
wheels repeating wheels.

A truck—
reluctant farmer
but darkness dived back
into darkness
the tunnel opened to receive him
an evil spirit
sucked back into a bottle.
The refuge became the trap.

Yet however long she lives
under the smooth brown hair
behind the blue eyes
he will keep coming

black
up out of the innocent golden ground
and in all her dreams
he will spin forever like the tumbled wheel
dust devil
wicked dervish
rising and twisting from the hole
as he tears her sleep.

1985

ELIZABETH SMART
1913–1986

The Muse: His & Hers

His pampered Muse
Knew no veto.
Hers lived
In a female ghetto.

When his Muse cried
He replied
Loud and clear
Yes! Yes! I'm waiting here.

Her Muse screamed
But children louder.
Then which strength
Made her prouder?

Neither. Either
Pushed and shoved
With the strength of the loved
And the unloved,

Clashed, rebuked:
All was wrong.
(Can you put opposites
Into a song?)

Kettles boiling!
Cobwebs coiling!

Doorbells ringing!
Needs haranguing!

Her Muse called
In her crowded ear.
She heard but had
Her dirty house to clear.

Guilt drove him *on*.
Guilt held her *down*.
(She hadn't a wife
To lean upon).

'The dichotomy
Was killing me,'
She said, 'till old age
Came to assuage.'

'Now! Muse, Now!
You can have your way!
(Now . . . what was it
I wanted to say?)'

Used, abused,
And not amused
The mind's gone blank—
Is it life you have to thank?

Stevie, the Emilys,
Mrs Woolf
By-passed the womb
And kept the Self.

But she said, 'Try
And see if it's true
(And without cheating)
My Muse can do.'

Can women do?
Can women make?
When the womb rests
Animus awake?

Pale, it must be,
Starved and thin,
Like hibernating bear,
Too weak to begin

To roar with authority
Poems in the spring
So late in the autumn
Of their suffering.

Those gaps! It's decades
Of lying low;
Earth-quaked, deep-frozen
Mind askew.

Is it too late
At sixty-eight?
O fragile flesh
Reanimate!

Eschew, true woman,
Any late profligacy
Squandered on the loving of people
And other irrelevancy,

Useful in the dark
Inarticulacy,
But drop it like poison now
If you want poetry.

Let the doorbell ring
Let the fire men
Put out the fire
Or light it up again.

Sheepish and shamefaced
At nine a.m.
Till the Muse commands
Her ritual hymn,

See lucky man
Get off his knee,

And hear now his roar
Of authority!

This test-case woman
Could also be
Just in time for
A small cacophany,

A meaningful scream
Between folded womb and grave,
A brief respite
From the enclave.

1982

Rose Died

Unstoppable blossom
above my rotting daughter.
Under the evil healing
bleeding, bleeding.

There was no way to explain
the godly law; pain.
For your leaping in greeting,
my failure, my betrayal,

shame for my cagey ways,
protective carapace;
blame for my greeting leaping
over your nowhere place.

Spring prods, I respond
to ancient notes that birds sing;
but the smug survivor says this is *after* the suffering,
a heavenly lift, an undeserved reward.

Your irreversible innocence
thought heaven now, and eternal,
was surprised, overwhelmed,
by the painful roughly presented bill,

the hateful ways of the ungenerous.
But, loving the unsuspecting flower,

could love urge bitchiness
as a safe protective covering?

O forgive, forgive, forgive,
as I know you would,
that my urgent live
message to you failed.

Two sins will jostle forever, and humble me
beneath my masked heart:
it was my job to explain the world;
it was my job to get the words right.

I tried, oh, I tried, I did try,
I biked through gales,
brought hugs, kisses,
but no explanation for your despair, your desperate Why.

With its smile-protected face,
my survival-bent person
is hurtled on by its nasty lucky genes,
its selfish reason,

and greets the unstoppable blossom
above my rotting daughter
but forever and ever within
is bleeding, bleeding.

1982

GWLADYS DOWNES
b. 1915

Cannibal Speech

The beat of the waves
is the beat of my layered breath,
the cormorant's most ancient skull
my own
stiff feathers pull new air
in black sacs, after the dive,
I hear
wind in the hollow bones

the breathing tide
is the pulse of my ancored heart
sun-watcher
whipped by the murderous moon
a quickening rhythm in fright
when the greedy bill
streaks down
strikes deep
for black-barred golden fish
to be tossed in air
to be swallowed alive
from a deadhead's side
in silver glitter of noon

eaten alive
my own, my own
eaten alive my own

1978

Flotsam at Rose Point

A brave boy beareth the flukes away—
after three days
no blood is criminal in these Islands

where we offer our faces
to the glittering spite of the midday sea
our vulnerable eyes

but do not admit a distant destruction
moon arcs of madness
gashing of green boughs

admitting it we should be wholly lost
in quicksands waiting by the river's mouth
unstable dunes

no perfect shells lie angled in these stones
but we are permitted to gather agates
of a certain luminosity

our real care, searching heads down over dry salt
is to avoid the haunted eyes
beyond the sun

'We have survived'—your voice against the wind
as though the end were
breath only, bitter air

binding us to knives and whale and running boy
and brilliant fingers torn apart by light,
the strange rebirth of suns.

1980

Stone Garden With Wasp

The landscape around has already
composed itself: to shift a cloud,
a roof diagonal, distort a tree
or change from East to West the delicate
angles of hills
would violate a truth, deny a poised
part of the whole,
and so, all.

Buddha lies among the mountains
in a position of rest
and these spare rocks, a stone calligraphy
elegantly disposed in a dry place
seem balanced too, but yet
unnatural—surely an invisible someone
wielding his bamboo rake
fans out the pebbled ground.

who would have expected the red pool, sulphurous,
fuming at the lip of the garden
or a tiny, black-striped killer
waiting in pungent mist?

Kyoto, October, 1984

1984

On the Sundeck

This swollen sac was once
my left hand
the wasp and I invisible
surprise to each other
yet the hurt from a desperate
wind-spun thing, caught on a skirt
carries no blame

You too. Not quite.
What was surprise
was the untold comfort
of the exchange, mature sweetness
like an Anjou pear or a perfectly
ripened apple—the rest
delayed pain, slow poison

Curiously, my right hand
continues to function, and my heart too
which lurched to a stop
but now moves strangely in a new accord,
healing itself, rebuilding cells,
almost restoring shape
round the bones of my bitten hand

1986

P.K. PAGE
b. 1916

The Stenographers

After the brief bivouac of Sunday,
their eyes, in the forced march of Monday to Saturday,
hoist the white flag, flutter in the snow-storm of paper,
haul it down and crack in the mid-sun of temper.

In the pause between the first draft and the carbon
they glimpse the smooth hours when they were children—
the ride in the ice-cart, the ice-man's name,
the end of the route and the long walk home;

remember the sea where floats at high tide
were sea marrows growing on the scatter-green vine
or spools of grey toffee, or wasps' nests on water;
remember the sand and the leaves of the country.

Bell rings and they go and the voice draws their pencil
like a sled across snow; when its runners are frozen
rope snaps and the voice then is pulling no burden
but runs like a dog on the winter of paper.

Their climates are winter and summer—no wind
for the kites of their hearts—no wind for a flight;
a breeze at the most, to tumble them over
and leave them like rubbish—the boy-friends of blood.

In the inch of the noon as they move they are stagnant.
The terrible calm of the noon is their anguish;
the lip of the counter, the shapes of the straws
like icicles breaking their tongues, are invaders.

Their beds are their oceans—salt water of weeping
the waves that they know—the tide before sleep;
and fighting to drown they assemble their sheep
in columns and watch them leap desks for their fences
and stare at them with their own mirror-worn faces.

In the felt of the morning the calico-minded,
sufficiently starched, insert papers, hit keys,
efficient and sure as their adding machines;
yet they weep in the vault, they are taut as net curtains
stretched upon frames. In their eyes I have seen
the pin men of madness in marathon trim
race round the track of the stadium pupil.

1946

Stories of Snow

Those in the vegetable rain retain
an area behind their sprouting eyes
held soft and rounded with the dream of snow
precious and reminiscent as those globes—
souvenir of some never-nether land—

which hold their snow-storms circular, complete,
high in a tall and teakwood cabinet.

In countries where the leaves are large as hands
where flowers protrude their fleshy chins
and call their colours,
an imaginary snow-storm sometimes falls
among the lilies.
And in the early morning one will waken
to think the glowing linen of his pillow
a northern drift, will find himself mistaken
and lie back weeping.
And there the story shifts from head to head,
of how in Holland, from their feather beds
hunters arise and part the flakes and go
forth to the frozen lakes in search of swans—
the snow-light falling white along their guns,
their breath in plumes.
While tethered in the wind like sleeping gulls
ice-boats wait the raising of their wings
to skim the electric ice at such a speed
they leap jet strips of naked water,
and how these flying, sailing hunters feel
air in their mouths as terrible as ether.
And on the story runs that even drinks
in that white landscape dare to be no colour;
how flasked and water clear, the liquor slips
silver against the hunters' moving hips.
And of the swan in death these dreamers tell
of its last flight and how it falls, a plummet,
pierced by the freezing bullet
and how three feathers, loosened by the shot,
descend like snow upon it.
While hunters plunge their fingers in its down
deep as a drift, and dive their hands
up to the neck of the wrist
in that warm metamorphosis of snow
as gentle as the sort that woodsmen know
who, lost in the white circle, fall at last
and dream their way to death.

And stories of this kind are often told
in countries where great flowers bar the roads

with reds and blues which seal the route to snow—
as if, in telling, raconteurs unlock
the colour with its complement and go
through to the area behind the eyes
where silent, unrefractive whiteness lies.

1946

After Rain

The snails have made a garden of green lace:
broderie anglaise from the cabbages,
chantilly from the choux-fleurs, tiny veils—
I see already that I lift the blind
upon a woman's wardrobe of the mind.

Such female whimsy floats about me like
a kind of tulle, a flimsy mesh,
while feet in gum boots pace the rectangles—
garden abstracted, geometry awash—
an unknown theorem argued in green ink,
dropped in the bath.
Euclid in glorious chlorophyll, half drunk.

I none too sober slipping in the mud
where rigged with guys of rain
the clothes-reel gauche
as the rangey skeleton of some
gaunt delicate spidery mute
is pitched as if
listening;
while hung from one thin rib
a silver web—
its infant, skeletal, diminutive,
now sagged with sequins, pulled ellipsoid,
glistening.

I suffer shame in all these images.
The garden is primeval, Giovanni
in soggy denim squelches by my hub
over his ruin,
shakes a doleful head.
But he so beautiful and diademmed,

his long Italian hands so wrung with rain
I find his ache exists beyond my rim
and almost weep to see a broken man
made subject to my whim.

O choir him, birds, and let him come to rest
within this beauty as one rests in love,
till pears upon the bough
encrusted with
small snails as pale as pearls
hang golden in
a heart that knows tears are a part of love.

And choir me too to keep my heart a size
larger than seeing, unseduced by each
bright glimpse of beauty striking like a bell,
so that the whole may toll,
its meaning shine
clear of the myriad images that still—
do what I will—encumber its pure line.

1956

Another Space

Those people in a circle on the sand
are dark against its gold
turn like a wheel
revolving in a horizontal plane
whose axis—do I dream it?—
vertical
invisible
immeasurably tall
rotates a starry spool.

Yet *if* I dream
why in the name of heaven are fixed parts
within me set in motion
like a poem?

Those people in a circle reel me in.
Down the whole length of golden beach I come

willingly pulled by their rotation
slow
as a moon pulls waters
on a string
their turning circle winds around its rim.

I see them there in three dimensions yet
their height implies another space
their clothes'
surprising chiaroscuro postulates
a different spectrum.
What kaleidoscope
does air construct
that all their movements make a compass rose
surging and altering?
I speculate
on some dimension I can barely guess.

Nearer I see them dark-skinned.
They are dark. And beautiful.
Great human sunflowers spinning in a ring
cosmic as any bumble-top
the vast
procession of the planets in their dance.
And nearer still I seem them—'a Chagall'—
each fiddling on an instrument—its strings
of some black woollen fibre
and its bow—feathered—
an arrow almost.
                    Arrow *is*.

For now the headman—one step forward—shoots
(or does he bow or does he lift a kite
up and over the bright pale dunes of air?)
to strike the absolute centre of my skull
my absolute centre somehow
with such skill
such staggering lightness
that the blow is love.

And something in me melts.
It is as if a glass partition melts—
or something I had always thought was glass—

some pane that halved my heart
is proved, in its melting, ice.

And to-fro all the atoms pass
in bright osmosis
hitherto
in stasis locked
where now a new
direction opens like an eye.

1974

After Reading Albino Pheasants

For Pat Lane

Pale beak . . . pale eye . . . the dark imagination
flares like magnesium. Add but *pale flesh*
and I am lifted to a weightless world:
watered cerulean, chrome-yellow (light)
and green, veronese—if I remember—a soft wash
recalls a summer evening sky.

At Barro de Navidad we watched the sky
fade softly like a bruise. Was it imagination
that showed us Venus phosphorescent in a wash
of air and ozone?—a phosphorescence flesh
wears like a mantle in bright moonlight,
a natural skin-tone in that other world.

Why should I wish to escape this world?
Why should three phrases alter the colour of the sky
the clarity, texture even, of the light?
What is there about the irrepressible imagination
that the adjective *pale* modifying *beak, eye* and *flesh*
can set my sensibilities awash?

If with my thickest brush I were to lay a wash
of thinnest watercolour I could make a world
as unlike my own dense flesh
as the high-moon midsummer sky;
but it would not catch at my imagination
or change the waves or particles of light

yet *pale* can tip the scales, make light
this heavy planet. If I were to wash
everything I own in mercury, would imagination
run rampant in that suddenly silver world—
free me from gravity, set me floating sky-
ward—thistledown—permanently disburdened of my flesh?

Like cygnets hatched by ducks, our minds and flesh
are imprinted early—what to me is light
may be dark to one born under a sunny sky.
And however cool the water my truth won't wash
without shrinking except in its own world
which is one part matter, nine parts imagination.

I fear flesh which blocks imagination,
the light of reason which constricts the world.
Pale beak . . . pale eye . . . pale flesh . . . My sky's awash.

1981

Deaf-Mute in the Pear Tree

His clumsy body is a golden fruit
pendulous in the pear tree

Blunt fingers among the multitudinous buds

Adriatic blue the sky above and through
the forking twigs

Sun ruddying tree's trunk, his trunk
his massive head thick-nobbed with burnished curls
tight-clenched in bud

(Painting by Generalić. Primitive.)

I watch him prune with silent secateurs

Boots in the crotch of branches shift their weight
heavily as oxen in a stall

Hear small inarticulate mews from his locked mouth
a kitten in a box

Pear clippings fall
                    soundlessly on the ground
Spring finches sing
                    soundlessly in the leaves

A stone. A stone in ears and on his tongue

Through palm and fingertip he knows the tree's
quick springtime pulse

Smells in its sap the sweet incipient pears

Pale sunlight's choppy water glistens on
his mutely snipping blades

and flags and scraps of blue
above him make regatta of the day

But when he sees his wife's foreshortened shape
sudden and silent in the grass below
uptilt its face to him

then air is kisses, kisses

stone dissolves

his locked throat finds a little door

and through it feathered joy
flies screaming like a jay

1985

A Little Fantasy

*'I send you a very well-constructed Kaleidoscope,
a recently invented Toy.'*
          —LETTER FROM JAMES MURRAY TO BYRON, 1818

So—Murray to Byron in Italy
when B. was falling in love again. In love.
Teresa this time. Guiciolli.
What a gift

to view her through that tube!
Her palms, sand dollars—
pale, symmetrical—
changed with his breathing
into petalled stars.
Four hearts her mouth, then eight,
a single flower
become a bunch
to kiss and kiss and kiss
and kiss a fourth time.
What a field of mouths!
Her navel—curling, complex—
shells and pearls
quadrupling for him
and her soft hair—ah,
the flat, sweet plait of it
beneath the glass—
a private hair brooch
such as ladies wear
pinned to their *peau de soie*.

Byron is breathing heavily
the tube—a lover's perfect toy—
weighting his palm.
'Quite a celestial kaleidoscope.'*
But Murray demands more cantos.
(Damn the man!)
Oh, multiple Teresa,
Don Juan calls.

1987

* *Don Juan*, XCIII

ELIZABETH GOURLAY
b. 1917

Bonsai, Haiku, a Seashell

I have seen a tree
ten inches tall resplendent
with tiny blue plums

I have read a poem
seventeen sounds redolent
of jasmine and love

once in mid-winter
I was offered a present
small brown and white shell

mollusk in water
most magically rent
grew into a flower

dear sloe-eyed artists
let me state this   there can be
no phoenix too frequent

1969

At the Gallery, San Francisco

the skull was there, of course, from the beginning

on what then
                    did the vision pend

                                        the light?
                                        the mind?

at first quick sight
the huge black arch
the cubed gold altar
the white cowled monks
before it bowing . . .

yet there was something
something dark one did not love. . . .

for I shivered
and my tongue hurt
and in my mind
a rook pulled at a gnarled root. . . .

                    turn

          walk swiftly

                    back
          three pictures back

                         to Balthus

          young girl before the mirror
          musing. . . .

not till afterwards
in the catalogue
did the Death Head show

                    and I saw
                    the whole painting
                    the hallucinating vision
                    the cracked gold cranium
                    its monks' teeth grinning. . . .

the skull was there, of course, from the beginning. . . .

1969

Rosencrantz and Guildenstern Are Dead

Rosencrantz and Guildenstern are dead
are dead
are dead
they did not die for love
unless, perhaps, obliquely
would they have sent the Messenger
if the King had not been eager
to take the Queen to bed?

they died
it was the time for
only the Player lasts
we all poor fools chew poppy

the black seed springs with birth
why truth?   where's guilt?   what's love for?
and whence the spiralled dust?
the King the Queen the Prince too
they paid the piper, yes
but who blows notes forever
skulls, hearts are easy cracked

there's blood there's bread and crust is
there's curds and whey and dance
when Guilden put his hand up
he felt the norther's blast
and was he then dead lucky?
or was he dead, by chance?
in sand or clay, by gold or lead,
eventually all coins must
flip down upon their heads

1969

Poem for a Poet Friend

I send you greeting
small colored postcard   painting
by Hiroshige

two blue-clad women
kneel dip their linen
deep in moonlit sea

look how rhythmically
they beat white sheets beneath this
forbidding mountain

see how their mouths fly
open   yes, they are singing
singers, like you, me

two ageing women
bereft of lovers, children
still making   music

what do they sing of?
round moon, the tides, the bitter
mountain, toppling wave. . . .

1988

MIRIAM WADDINGTON
b. 1917

Icons

Suddenly
in middle age
instead of withering
into blindness
and burying myself
underground
I grow delicate
and fragile
superstitious;
I carry icons
I have begun
to worship
images.

I take them out
and prop them up
on bureau tops
in hotel rooms
in Spain
I study them
in locked libraries
in Leningrad
I untie them
from tourist packages
in Italy
they warm me
in the heatless winters
of London in the
hurry-up buses
of Picadilly.

my icons are not
angels or holy
babies they have
nothing to do
with saints or
madonnas, they
are mostly of
seashores summer
and love which I no
longer believe in
but I still believe
in the images,
I still preserve
the icons:

a Spanish factory
worker talks to me
in a street behind
the cathedral he
offers me *un poco
amor*, the scars on
his hand, his wounded
country and the black-
jacketed police; he
touches me on the
arm and other places,
and the alcoholic
in the blazing square
drinks brandy, confides
that fortunes can still
be made in Birmingham
but he has a bad
lung is hard of
hearing and owns
an apartment in Palma.

in Montreal a man
in a white shirt
with his sleeves
rolled up is reading
a book and waiting
for me in a room

with the door ajar,
the light falls
through the open
door the book
falls from his
open hand and he
stands up and
looks at me with
open eyes.

of course I know
these are only
icons; there is
no such thing
as love left in
the world but
there is still
the image of it
which doesn't let
me wither into
blindness which
doesn't let me
bury myself
underground which
doesn't let me
say yes to the
black leather police
or the empty libraries
or the lonely rooms
or the foggy windows
of cold London buses.

the world is getting
dark but I carry
icons   I remember
the summer
I will never forget
the light.

1969

Moscow Roses

You send me roses
from Moscow a
postcard telling
about winter and
being stranded in
a hotel far from
the apple market.

You remind me
to feel helpless
and suddenly I'm
surrounded by
empty fur coats
who have lost
the people who
used to wear them.

1972

Ten Years and More

When my husband
lay dying a mountain
a lake three
cities ten years
and more
lay between us:

There were our
sons my wounds
and theirs,
despair loneliness,
handfuls of un-
hammered nails
pictures never
hung all

The uneaten
meals and unslept
sleep; there was
retirement, and

worst of all
a green umbrella
he can never
take back.

I wrote him a
letter but all
I could thing of
to say was: do you
remember Severn
River, the red canoe
with the sail
and lee-boards?

I was really saying
for the sake of our
youth and our love
I forgave him for
everything
and I was asking him
to forgive me too.

1976

MARGARET AVISON
b. 1918

Snow

Nobody stuffs the world in at your eyes.
The optic heart must venture: a jail-break
And re-creation. Sedges and wild rice
Chase rivery pewter. The astonished cinders quake
With rhizomes. All ways through the electric air
Trundle candy-bright disks; they are desolate
Toys if the soul's gates seal, and cannot bear,
Must shudder under, creation's unseen freight.
But soft, there is snow's legend: colour of mourning
Along the yellow Yangtze where the wheel
Spins an indifferent stasis that's death's warning.
Asters of tumbled quietness reveal

Their petals. Suffering this starry blur
The rest may ring your change, sad listener.

1960

The World Still Needs

Frivolity is out of season.
Yet, in this poetry, let it be admitted
The world still needs piano-tuners
And has fewer, and more of these
Gray fellows prone to liquor
On an unlikely Tuesday, gritty with wind,
When somewhere, behind windows,
A housewife stays for him until the
      Hour of the uneasy bridge-club cocktails
      And the office rush at the groceteria
      And the vesper-bell and lit-up buses passing
      And the supper trays along the hospital corridor,
Suffering from
Sore throat and dusty curtains.

Not all alone on the deserted boathouse
Or even on the prairie freight
(The engineer leaned out, watchful and blank
And had no Christmas worries
Mainly because it was the eve of April),
Is like the moment
When the piano in the concert-hall
Finds texture absolute, a single solitude
For those hundreds in rows, half out of overcoats,
Their eyes swimming with sleep.

From this communal cramp of understanding
Springs up suburbia, where every man would build
A clapboard in a well of Russian forest
With yard enough for a high clothesline strung
To a small balcony . . .
A woman whose eyes shine like evening's star
Takes in the freshblown linen
While sky a lonely wash of pink is still

reflected in brown mud
Where lettuces will grow, another spring.

1960

New Year's Poem

The Christmas twigs crispen and needles rattle
Along the windowledge.
        A solitary pearl
Shed from the necklace spilled at last week's party
Lies in the suety, snow-luminous plainness
Of morning, on the windowledge beside them.
And all the furniture that circled stately
And hospitable when these rooms were brimmed
With perfumes, furs, and black-and-silver
Crisscross of seasonal conversation, lapses
Into its previous largeness.
        I remember
Anne's rose-sweet gravity, and the stiff grave
Where cold so little can contain;
I mark the queer delightful skull and crossbones
Starlings and sparrows left, taking the crust,
And the long loop of winter wind
Smoothing its arc from dark Arcturus down
To the bricked corner of the drifted courtyard,
And the still windowledge.
        Gentle and just pleasure
It is, being human, to have won from space
This unchill, habitable interior
Which mirrors quietly the light
Of the snow, and the new year.

1960

The Swimmer's Moment

For everyone
The swimmer's moment at the whirlpool comes,
But many at that moment will not say
'This is the whirlpool, then.'
By their refusal they are saved

From the black pit, and also from contesting
The deadly rapids, and emerging in
The mysterious, and more ample, further waters.
And so their bland-blank faces turn and turn
Pale and forever on the rim of suction
They will not recognize.
Of those who dare the knowledge
Many are whirled into the ominous centre
That, gaping vertical, seals up
For them an eternal boon of privacy,
So that we turn away from their defeat
With a despair, not for their deaths, but for
Ourselves, who cannot penetrate their secret
Nor even guess at the anonymous breadth
Where one or two have won:
(The silver reaches of the estuary).

1960

Voluptuaries and Others

That Eureka of Archimedes out of his bath
Is the kind of story that kills what it conveys;
Yet the banality is right for that story, since it is not a
  communicable one
But just a particular instance of
The kind of lighting up of the terrain
That leaves aside the whole terrain, really,
But signalizes, and compels, an advance in it.
Such an advance through a be-it-what-it-may but take-it-not-
  quite-as-given locale:
Probably that is the core of being alive.
The speculation is not a concession
To limited imaginations. Neither is it
A constrained voiding of the quality of immanent death.
Such near values cannot be measured in values
Just because the measuring
Consists in that other kind of lighting up
That shows the terrain comprehended, as also its containing
  space,
And wipes out adjectives, and all shadows
    (or, perhaps, all but shadows).

The Russian made a movie of a dog's head
Kept alive by blood controlled by physics, chemistry, equip-
     ment, and
Russian women scientists in cotton gowns with writing tablets.
The heart lay on a slab midway in the apparatus
And went phluff, phluff.
Like the first kind of illumination, that successful experiment
Can not be assessed either as conquest or as defeat.
But it is living, creating the chasm of creation,
Contriving to cast only man to brood in it, further.

History makes the spontaneous jubilation at such moments
     less and less likely though,
And that story about Archimedes does get into public school
     textbooks.

1960

July Man

Old, rain-wrinkled, time-soiled, city-wise, morning man
whose weeping is for the dust of the elm-flowers
and the hurting motes of time,
rotted with rotting grape,
sweet with the fumes,
puzzled for good by fermented potato-
peel out of the vat of the times,
turned out and left
in this grass-patch, this city-gardener's place
under the buzzing populace's
square shadows, and the green shadows
of elm and ginkgo and lime
(planted for Sunday strollers and summer evening
families, and for those
bird-cranks with bread-crumbs
and crumpled umbrellas who come
while the dew is wet on the park, and beauty
is fan-tailed, gray and dove gray, aslant, folding in
from the white fury of day).

In the sound of the fountain
you rest, at the cinder-rim, on your bench.

The rushing river of cars
makes you a stillness, a pivot, a heart-stopping
blurt, in the sorrow
of the last rubbydub swig, the searing, and
stone-jar solitude lost, and yet,
and still—wonder (for good now) and
trembling:

    The too much none of us knows
    is weight, sudden sunlight, falling
    on your hands and arms, in your lap,
    all, all, in time.

1966

In a Season of Unemployment

These green painted park benches are
all new. The Park Commissioner had them
planted.
Sparrows go on
having dust baths at the edge of
the park maple's shadow, just where
the bench is cemented down, planted
and then cemented.

    Not a breath moves
    this newspaper.
    I'd rather read it by the Lapland sun at midnight. Here we're
    bricked in early by a
    stifling dark.

On that bench a man in a
pencil-striped white shirt
keeps his head up and steady.

    The newspaper-astronaut says
    'I feel excellent under the condition of weightlessness.'
And from his bench a
scatter of black bands in the hollow air
ray out—too quick for the eye—
and cease.

'Ground observers watching him on a TV circuit said
At the time of this report he
was smiling,' Moscow ra-
dio reported.
I glance across at him, and mark that
he is feeling
excellent too, I guess, and
weightless and
'smiling.'

1966

The Mourner

'Because the windows were boarded up
on us, though when the wind
blew in this dry tree-scaley scruff
or the swimmer's morning freshness, we can, now,
not securely remember,
but because the windows were
boards, one pencil beam
no longer diffused, no longer confusable
with the virtues of visibility,
but purely, narrowly,
compellingly
itself, is evidence that there is
Tree. Morning. Freshness. Even though
the windows have been boarded
up on
us,'
told the Mourner, moving
down the grass-blowing years, marking
a day.

1966

Unspeakable

The beauty of the unused
        (the wheatear among birds, or
                    stonechat)
the unused in houses (as a

      portion of low roof swept by the
          buttery leaves of a pear tree
          where a manx cat is
          discovered—just now—blinking his
              sunned Arctic sea-eyes in the
              sun-play)
the beauty of the
      unused in one I know, of
      excellent indolence
          from season into
             skywide wintering
should be
confidently, as it is
copious and new into the morning,
celebrated.

1966

ELIZABETH BREWSTER
b. 1922

In Wellington, For Katherine Mansfield

A cold, sullen afternoon in Wellington—
late March—late autumn—
Saturday afternoon, with all the shops closed
so tight I can't even buy a postcard

in your home town, K.M.
(born Kathleen Beauchamp
in this city of ugly buildings
and beautiful bays)

I have taken the tourist bus
up all those winding streets
where the houses perch on cliffs
like nests above the water
and down roads past craggy beaches
where the waves dash foaming
against the shore

(On a dull street in the New Town
the driver said,
'This street's called Mansfield
after the famous poet';
and I knew without asking
she had never read your work)

And now, the drive over, nothing to do,
tired of walking
through windy streets in the half-drizzle
past all the shuttered shops and lunchrooms,
I come back to my hotel on Lambton Quay
(where you once stood reading
one of your first stories
in a newspaper)
I snuggle from the chill
under the eiderdown,
propped up with pillows,
reading scraps of your letters

written also in hotel-rooms
alone in foreign countries
while you cuddled a hot-water bottle
or a fat
Dickens novel
to drive away the nightmare
or jotted the price of your meals
in the back of your notebook
next to the hints for stories.

Last night there was thunder
and lightning flashing.
There were huge gusts of wind
and the rain came by bucketsful

and there were people screaming in the street
outside my window
as if for help or in anger

And I thought of you torn out of life
pretending happiness and serenity
but really screaming (silently) for help,

angry, fearful, not sure you were beloved,
not satisfied with your stories

('I want much more material'
you said, 'I am tired of my little stories
like birds bred in cages')

wanting life, health, gardens, babies
to replace those lost,
wanting to see New Zealand again,
wanting time, time, a whole lifetime.

And while you were dying
gasping in your eagerness for life
I was a child in the cradle
mindless as a plant
floating in air
knowing nothing
caring for nothing
the pale January sun touching
my small fingers clenched
above the white wool coverlet
as I breathed in
breathed out
easily

no trouble at all

1982

Reading Old Poetry Notebooks

trying to salvage
a line here, an image there,
perhaps sometimes even a whole poem
with only a few changes

it's as if I were thriftily looking
through an old wardrobe
from the seventies, sixties, fifties
for reusable clothing

taking a tuck here
letting out a seam there,
wishing I had more of this precious bolt
of sage-green shot silk,
regretting the moth holes in the wool cardigan
the missing snaps
the tarnished buckle.

Much of this cloth
could only be reused
for making patchwork quilts:
a painstaking art
requiring accurate vision
nimble fingers
the most consummate
skill with the needle

beyond me, perhaps

yet the thrift inherited
from mother, grandmother, aunts
makes me fondle
the old garments wistfully:
and something more than thrift—
a yearning to hold on,
to make a pattern
from these discarded scraps;

a memory of how I felt
the April afternoon
I wore the green silk
all those years ago,
how someone I loved
said I looked well in it

and the Christmas like an April
in Indiana
when I wore the red wool dress
with its blue butterfly buttons,
was half drunk
with wine and laughter

(How I loved that dress
even after it was stained
and had lost a button)

and there is a dress
of striped cotton
I wore by the bedside
of my dying father

a linen handkerchief
splotched with blood
from a wound or nosebleed
or perhaps only red ink.

It's my life here
I think
in these clothes
these notebooks

my ink on the page, the handkerchief

my blood

1982

RONA MURRAY
b. 1924

To Angels

Now leave me alone.

This room has laths that are thin
and floors worn almost through
into the world below.

How may this place—
the Old King on the wall
the wine on the table
the pottery birds
the dictionary with all the meanings
of all the words—
bear the weight of your multiple feet?

Sometimes suddenly I see one of your faces:
then the rain on the window stops
but immediately the moment is gone
ravished with sensation that cannot be named.

You stand always at the periphery of vision,
demanding I abandon the skin
that holds my bones into some kind of pattern.

1968

The Lizard

Do you remember the lizard?

I remember the dark man
squatting turbaned in the garden,
the hard hot earth,
the green parrots that came suddenly
in thousands out of nowhere
into the green peepul tree.

Do you remember the lizard?

I remember the three-fingered man;
he stood under a banyan tree
circled with cement to keep away snakes.
He was strange, they said;
he did not always know what he did.
One day when the dog lay still in the heat
and bananas hung on the banana tree
he was jailed out of the garden.
To me he was not strange.

Do you remember the lizard?

I remember the baby.
It had been left on the floor
of a white and empty house
on a hill across the bed of the dried river.
When they brought it to
my young and dancing mother
its skin was pitted by lime.

It was a girl.
They fed her milk with an eye-dropper.

Do you remember the lizard?

I remember the porcupine quills
the rabbit fur
the snake my father killed
the scarlet poinsettia growing high
into a pitiless sky.

Do you remember the lizard?

Under the jacaranda tree
the dark man in his white turban
cut the lizard into two pieces
across the middle;
two clawed feet and a tail
scrabbled under some leaves,
two clawed feet and a bright, unblinking head
went in another direction.
The parrots were making a great noise
and the man said,
staring intently at a smear of colourless blood,
—You see, it does not hurt him;
he is not dead.

1974

Exorcism

Old fathers
will you forever
encrust yourselves
        barnacles upon
        my skull?

                Old mothers
                will you stare
                endless out
                caged between
                the ribby structures
                of my chest

                    peering at
                    the course
                    I try to chart?

I move weighted
in waters
that would founder
better craft:
                    ancestral blood
                    reaching into gales or shoals
                    I would   to find my scrap of self   avoid

Now take your ghostly breath
and whistle down the wind
before you reef my trial
or flotsam it in heaving seas
with nothing left of me
but in my turn
                    to be avaricious eyes
                    locked between
                    the ribs
                    of my own distant children's
                    enterprise

                            or

                    hungry tentacles barnacled
                        into their skulls

1981

COLLEEN THIBAUDEAU
b. 1925

Poem

I do not want only
The shy child with the shock of slippery wheatlike hair
Standing alone after her first communion
By the white picket fence,
She is light and airy
She is for once still and stilled her shrill voice,

She is like a beefy window curtain
Or a lacy Breughel
And must be trained in the right way
Lest she twist and turn like a very poem.
I want the others too.
I want the baby in—
He who sits under the hollyhocks
His behind the exact same shade as the Purple King hollyhock at
    the very top.
I want too the neighbour looking over with a leer
At the big sister got up to look like Rita Hayworth
White as white as in a restaurant.
I want the young Socialist on the corner with his cough
I want the mother
Though they tell me she lies in the churchyard
That is halfway up Montreal Mountain.
I want the man who sits on the steps of the Mayfair Washing
    Machine Co.
This morning and every morning
Wearing a dirty hockey sweater and holding his head in his hands.

And I too
After adjusting the focus
I shall go just as natural among them all;
Why must the lover and the sufferer be out?
I do not want the shy child only
Aloof for the one minute of her life;
I want it to be like a lacy Breughel.

1977

The Green Family

I will begin to delineate the green family.
Under the shade of the mother sat the father
small weedy and seedy
wearing his light hair daubed on his forehead;
he was a salvation army man, weekdays
he moved ashcans for the city.

His children were all mouths diligent with love of honey.
They could have spelled down anybody's child.
Sitting in the front row at the library hour

they let their darned black legs hang down,
all of them thin as water spiders, and the gold
dream of his trumpet kept them whole.

Summer sand could have held them
like five smooth stones. Off to one side
was the mother being a flowering-bush in her housedress.
They consulted about the special ride; at twilight
he took the three biggest ones aboard
that marvel of a varnished speedboat and went off in a wave.

He could not walk on water. When the shock came
he was a gallant giving his arm
in perfect faith to his three small daughters,
told them the longest story they had ever heard;
going along that hollow wooden walk by the lake
they came to the all-gold sugar bush of the tale.

The airforce dragged
him up pale as a weed-draped Shiva;
one of the other mothers told that she was knitting
a wee red jacket for her Rita that would have been
more mere red flesh though and no sort of preserver.
Henry had been an angel.

I cannot bring my heart to mourn
his unreturn,
nor can the remnant that remember him
remembering he looked last into the sun
that was a golden gabriel and sang him home.

1977

An Afternoon's Teasing . . .

On a day so hot that farm dogs, cats, geese, and goats
Had had enough and lay extended, letting millers at their coats,
Clocks at their feathers, burrs and docks gnarl and gather,
Mrs Burrows was out sitting teasing up wool in the garden grass.

Under the Duchess apple tree small yellowing leaves kept falling
Tent caterpillars kept spinning out their lavender wares, lolling

Cats on the parquet looked at Mrs Burrows larkily
Teasing out wool over the bright eyes of any birds to pass.

Mr Burrows was engaged out among the brown furrows, bleared
Before his eyes matted red-spattered berries appeared
Blending with sweat and flies came a violet storm threat,
That made all the ploughed field languid as a brown-tressed lass.

Abe Burrows turned in the field, rain was as certain
As his wishes, driving the tractor up, through the thick curtain
Of his thoughts it was a white girl-bride under an apple tree he
    caught
Sight of, not brown wrinkled Julia busily teasing wool in the grass.

Tired Abe took a long drink at the pump that quenched his vision
    well
But he still stood there musing when the first spears of rain fell
Ambushing Julia, who slowly gathered up her snowy teased wool,
Losing forever an old man's bearded face in the mass.

1977

Poem

A feeling of nightfall having been alone all day
May come by even five p.m. I put on scarves, gay gloves, leave
    them—
Papers, tomatoes, Morley Callaghan, the pictures (little clay
Chicken, Flower Vendor, the static redlegged horse)
Blessing what holds them in their course while I'm away.

Once in the tipsy shrug of a street I could cry aloud
Of something that tugs and bunts me against people and
    storefronts—
O to mash into piles of oranges, piles of pink Telys, into the
    crowd,
Combatting colour with a deep but china cheep, a Buy Come Buy,
    a redlegged neigh—
To leap with such inaudible clamour is always glamourous and
    proud.

1977

The Brown Family

All round the Browns stretched forty acres of potatoes.
They lived like squatters in my father's little chicken-house
That grew to lean-tos and then to a whole shack-town where
    married Browns
Slept God-knows-how hilled in the darkness all night long,
Mornings how rolled out to breakfast on the lawn
Sitting in crumbs and clover, their eyes still glozed over
With dufferish sleep, and all stuffing away like Eskimos.

Brown boys had greasy jeans and oilcloth school-bags made at
    home
And sneakers for quick escapes through orchard gates,
Tom had two left thumbs while Ted was tough and dumb, but
    there was much
Of army sadness to the way all their heads got furry as muskrats by
    March.
Well after meagre spells Fall was their full season when they
    dropped
Partridge, pheasant and squirrel—shooting as if they would never
    stop
As later they crazily shot up even the apple-trees at Caen.

Their sisters inevitably called Nellie or Lily were deliberately pale,
Silly incestuous little flirts whose frilly skirts were dirty
From every ditch in the country. On lonely country roads under
    the moon
Their sadness lit like incense their sweet ten-cent perfume.
But at hint of insult their cheeks took on fiery tints those summers
When they hired-out to cook. And their eyes often had that strange
    blue look
Of the blue willow plates round a rich farmer's plate-rail.

'What I can touch and take up in these two hands,' said Mrs
    Brown,
'Is what I trust!' Accordingly on the bashed piano and on the floor,
    dust
And rich potato-coloured light everywhere mingled: scraps, fronds,
    gourds,
Teazle, fossils, hazel wands, turkey feathers and furs . . . goods
All lovingly hers tangled. And all could be taken up, stroked,
    cajoled

In the same manner as her Old Man: for Mr Brown's heart was
    pure glossy gold
By tender handling, of all that's drossy, slowly, suvendibly,
    rendered down.

But as alike as Anna Pauker's brood so that it tears the heart to see
Was that last lot and will all Browns ever be,
Picking and pecking at life, scratching where something is cached.
What are they looking for? Not lots to eat or wear. Not lots in
    town.
Strangely, that same thing *we* want would satisfy a Brown—
Something of the sort God gives us every day
Something we can take up in our two hands and bear away.

1977

PHYLLIS GOTLIEB
b. 1926

Three-Handed Fugue

Into Suburbia between eight and nine
the army of cleaning-women marches,
knot-haired browbeaten
arbiters of mop and bucket, eaten
by acid lines about the mouth. Armpit-sweating
handmaidens of Godliness, they let down
great fuming freshets of hot water, pour
libations of Olddutch to the Allhigh
and praise Jehovah in terms of bleaches and starches.

Polisher and vacuum-cleaner roar
like the bellmouth of Moses at idolsfall
and MENE, MENE in noseprints on the windows
vanish, and TEKEL UPHARSIN the writing on the wall.

Burnished doorknobs sing
Hosannah! In white enamel
they build slender arches of worship, Bacchian eyries
of handworn wood, boneclean, glittering.

Exalted, stayed with cups of tea they make decorous
retreat by four.

As the golden light
burns through crystal panes, insidiously the mote
falls in the beam, turning like a feather.

And you and I, climbing the stairs by midnight
leave stubfilled ashtrays, islands in a sea of shards
and celebrating in criscrisp sheets together
pull down the house of cards.

1964

This One's on Me

1. The lives and times of Oedipus and Elektra
   began with bloodgrim lust and dark carnality
   but I was born next to the Neilson's factory
   where every piece is different, and that's how I got
   my individuality.

2. I lived on Gladstone Avenue,
   2 locations on Kingston Rd
   2 crescents, Tennis and Chaplin
   Xanadu, Timbuktu,
   Samarkand & Ampersand
   and many another exotic locality.

3. My grandparents came from the ghettos
   of Russia and Poland with no mementos
   one grandfather was a furrier, one a tailor,
   grey men in dark rooms tick tack to
   gether dry snuffy seams of fur and fibre
   my father managed a theatre

4. which one day (childhood reminiscence indicated) passing
   on a Sunday ride, we found
   the burglar alarm was ring
   alingaling
   out jumped my father and ran for the front door
   Uncle Louie ran for the back

siren scream down the cartrack Danforth
and churchbells ding dong ding
(ting a ling)
and brakescreech whooee
six fat squadcars filled with the finest
of the force of our fair city
brass button boot refulgent
and in their plainclothes too
greysuit felthat and flat black footed
and arrested Uncle Louie

Oh what a brannigan
what a brouhaha
while Mother and Aunt Gittel and me
sat in the car and shivered
delicious
ly

because a mouse bit through a wire.

5. For some the dance of the sugar-plum fairies
    means that.
    but the Gryphons and Gorgons of my dreams
    dance in the salon of Miss Peregrine Peers
    stony eyed, stone footed on Church Street
    up grey stairs
    where two doors down at Dr Weams I
    gnawed his smoky fingers and followed
    the convolutions of his twisted septum
    as he stretched and knotted little twines of silver
    on the rack of my oral cavity
    and all the while Miss Peregrine Peers
    tum tiddy tum tiddy TUM TUM TUM
    O Peregrine O Miss Peers
    I find you no longer in life's directories
    may you rest in peace
    and I do mean

6. Where, oh where are the lovely ladies who taught me
    to break the
    Hearts And trample the *Flowers* of the muses?

                                              Mrs Reeves

    gracile, a willow on a Chinese plate, who

winced with an indrawn gasp when I struck a wrong
note, or blew my nose in her handkerchief
absentmindedly?
Miss Marll, under whose tutelage icecubes
popped from the pores of my arm
pits and slid down to drop from my
ELBOWS HELD HIGH FINGERS CURVED ON THE KEYS
may you rot in hell
subtly, Miss Marll.

7. O child of the thirties
    of stonewarm porches and spiraea snowfalls
    in print cotton dress with matching panties hanging well down
    (the faded snapshot says)
    hand on the fender of the Baby Austin
    (feel the heat and glare)
    gaptooth grin to be converted by braces
    myopic eyes fit for glasses
    and tin ears waiting to be bent
    by the patient inexorable piano teacher
    the postered car advertises in innocence:
    LADIES OF LEISURE
    See it at the Eastwood Theatre, friends,
    next time 1930 rolls around.

1964

Late Gothic

From the window of my grandfather's
front room above the store I could see
over the asylum wall through the barred window
a madwoman raving, waving
pink arm sleeves. From the kitchen at the back
faceted skylights lay, grown quartz among the sooty
stalagmite chimneys. Two faces of despair.

My grandmother and grandfather cultivated
in the scoured yard of their love
a garden of forget-me.

My grandmother was a golden
turbulence, my goldwin, giver of all

lovehated vortex. Like all children I looked
twenty-five years later at her picture and found
the woman, monstrously coarse and obese
a drowned reaching beauty.

My grandfather, crumpled old Jew, read Hebrew
through a magnifying glass, crawled
to the park for sun, swore, told old tales
babbled of green fields and died.

My father sold that legendary
furniture for twelve dollars.
                        and we smelled the stench
of the furs the old man had made his shapeless coats of
and went down the narrow walled stair for the last time
into the bright street between the wall upflung
against the howling chimney of the madwoman's throat
on the one side
and the redbrick rampart of shoddy stores against the
reaching blackened arms of the chimneys on the other.

1964

Death's Head

at 3 a.m. I run my tongue
around my teeth (take in a breath)
(give out a breath) take one more step
approaching death. my teeth are firm
and hard and white (take in a breath)
incisors bite and molars grind
(give out a breath) the body lying
next to mine is sweet and warm
I've heard that worms (take in a breath)
don't really eat (give out a breath)
the coffin meat of human kind
and if they did I wouldn't mind
that's what I heard (take in a breath)
(and just in time) I think it's all
a pack of lies. I know my flesh
will end in slime. the streets are mean
and full of thieves. the children in
the sleeping rooms (give out a breath)

walk narrowly upon my heart
the animal beneath the cloth
submerged rises to any bait
of lust or fury, love or hate
(take in a breath) my orbic skull
is eminently frangible
so delicate a shell to keep
my brains from spillage. still my breath
goes in and out and nearer death

and yet I seem to get to sleep

1969

ANNE SZUMIGALSKI
b. 1926

Fishhawks

my son stands in waist-high water
the salt reddens his skin
out of his face spring wiry hairs
thickening to a beard
his arms have become wide and heavy

he splices rope
smells of the tar that blackens his fingers
he has learned to make his living from the sea

(the huge shadow of a bird
darkens the sand around us
I speak, say to you *look
at that rare creature
an osprey*)

further out from the shore
your daughter is a rock
jutting from the waves
she is rounded and hollow
within her is a sea-cave
her face is a pearly shell
a shining operculum

stoppers up her mouth
her singing is muffled, a murmur

the boy smiles
his semen darts out of him
a shoal of swift fishes
entering her secret place
he stretches out his finger
flicks away the shell plug from her mouth
so that she may cry out

you look at me, say
this has all happened far too quickly
we wade out   I say:
there is just time for us to bless them
but in that glance they have crossed the horizon
are washed away out of our sight

we two return to the beach
the salt water drips from us
making the dull shingles glisten
our wet clothes cling to our legs
behind us the sun is clouded
the sea is cold not splendid
I am a widow I tell you
but we are just strangers you reply

out there where the great bird hovers
mantling preparing to spiral
there is a faint wailing

1980

Shrapnel

shrapnel has torn the man's ribs apart
there is a shabby wound in his breast
his mouth opens innocently upon a cry

he wants to curse his enemies but cannot
for he sees them as striplings lying in the grass
each with a girl beneath him
the long grass full of clover and fieldherbs

waves gently in the heat
the men get up from the women
and buckle on their belts
the women just lie there looking up at the thundery sky
we are wounded with joy they tell each other
we are happy happy happy

the soldier sees this he hears all this
as he lies there asking the earth
is this my final place my own place
he glances upwards to where
the tops of the trees almost meet
there is just a small patch of empty sky showing
it must be spring for a bird with a straw in its beak
swoops down to a low bough   he tries to think
of the name of the bird
he tries to think of his own name
the name of his son who has learned to speak already
so his wife writes   he has seen the child only once
and that was more than a year ago

he tries to remember the colour of his wife's eyes
he sees only her frailty those little narrow birdbones
beneath the soft flesh
he wishes she was another woman
one easier to abandon   one calm and robust
with a wide smooth brow

but who could forget that pitiful teat
in the child's mouth
the curious maze of blue milkveins whose pattern
he traces in the dirt   his hand touches a broken brick
here was a house   now he remembers the collapse
of its walls

he licks his lips tasting for brickdust
he counts his strong teeth with his tongue
they are all there unchipped   he hears the bland
voice of the dentist telling him he has perfect bite

he shuts his eyes against the light but it shines on
through rosy lids which are the same colour exactly
as his wife's secret he wants to part her legs

and touch her glistening vermilion lining
now at last he understands
why he loves the bodies of women
more than the bodies of men   for pale skin covers
a man all over and only a wound can show his lining

carefully he passes his hands over his body
buttoned into its tunic of stiff drab wool
until he finds the hole in his chest
he thrusts in his fist to staunch the blood
a pulse beats close to his folded fingers
it is insistent and strong
it is pushing him away from himself

1983

The Bees

you speak in a dry voice of the sunburnt skin on the face of the woman
who tells through a mouthful of grit of an unpainted house scoured
by the sun where she stands on an old chair with a thin rag in her
hand trying to clean the window where dirt has lodged in the corners
of the frame

she tells of when you were a boy lying faceup in a field of many-
coloured clover set upon by bees their humm humm bumblebees
groundbees purring in their furry bodies you see them huge as cats
leaping from the clover flowers and chasing you down the gravel road
through a wire fence and into a field of tall green wheat where you
crouch breathless with your hands around the back of your neck trying
to ward off those darts from piercing the delicate flesh behind your
earlobes

the hum grows louder and louder it comes from overhead where one
lazy plane is flying and now the earth tilts so that the sky is below
you are falling into a pit of sky deeper than the slough deeper than
the well

slowly through space you fall more than a month you name the days
as you fall you write the names with a white pencil of smoke on the
walls of the sky

on the fourth sunday you see that at last you are approaching the plane
a silver insect not at all like a bee it is tin like a christmas present its
edges sharp as a toy car hood

after dinner you play in the yard with your new toy you don't need
winter boots because there is no snow *this is a black christmas* your
mother explains *it is dark all over there is a war on we must pray for peace*
and she ties her new red kerchief very tight under her chin

outside it is stony cold the pebbles under your feet are sharp you can
see the pointed stars they sting your eyes with their light the yard is
silvery not black you throw the tin plane up it falls into the trough
where a foal is drinking there is ice on the foal's lip

humm humm humm the airplane flies through the night the passengers
are singing as they fly *you are younger than you were in the summer* they
sing *you are getting younger all the time soon you will shrink down to a
baby small enough to get back into your mother you will ride inside her all
winter you will hear the squelch of the floormop you will hear the squeak of
the cloth as you try to clean the corners of the window*

while you were away while you were off in the sky the woman and
the house have crumbled and blown away now there is just one wall
left standing just one window with no glass through it you can see
the prairie and far away the crumpled riverbed under the window
stands an old chair with a rung missing and a stained cooking pot full
of rain where a bumblebee is collecting water for her family, they live
in a hole in the ground

and dryly you explain to your child how the sun is really an image
of our idea of the sun just as the prairie is a reflection of our need for
flatness *consider* you tell him *the clever dance of the bee which is in the
exact shape of her idea of distance*

1983

Fennec

my nibs and quills arranged before me on a stained deal table I am
designing the alphabet for a new language called in that tongue *speech
of the foxes* because the consonants fall on the ear like the yipping of

reynard in the henrun   because when a woman enunciates the vowels
they sound the human cry of a vixen in heat

precisely I fill in the empty eyes of the letters with slit-shaped green
ink *viridian* it says on the bottle *lamp black* on the tube I pick for the
pupils

with a blade I scrape flaky rust from the window-catch then spit and
a mix a reddish pigment brush between the letters cursive loops that
crouch and slink across the page

I'm weary with invention cannot find the strength to reject an idea
for punctuation: two small triangles a pair of pricked-up ears

1983

PHYLLIS WEBB
b. 1927

The Colour of the Light

I
On the apparent corner of two streets
a strange man shook
a blue cape above my head,
I saw it as the shaking sky
and was forthwith ravished.

II
A man bent to light a cigarette.
This was in the park
and I was passing through.
With what succinct ease he joins
himself to flame!
I passed by silently noting
how clear were the colours of pigeons
and how mysterious the animation of children
playing in trees.

III
When a strange man arrays
a dispassionate quality before
his public, the public may be deceived,

but a man's strange passion
thrusts deeper and deeper
into its fire of dispassionate
hard red gems.

IV
And the self is a grave
music will not mold
nor grief destroy;
yet this does not make refusal:
somehow . . . somehow . . .
shapes fall in a torrent of design
and over the violent space
assume a convention;
Or in the white, white, quivering
instability of love
we shake a world to order:
our prismed eyes divide such light
as this world dreams on
and rarely sees.

I thought I saw the pigeons in the trees . . .

1954

Poetics Against the Angel of Death

I am sorry to speak of death again
(some say I'll have a long life)
but last night Wordsworth's 'Prelude'
suddenly made sense—I mean the measure,
the elevated tone, the attitude
of private Man speaking to public men.
Last night I thought I would not wake again
but now with this June morning I run ragged to elude
The Great Iambic Pentameter
who is the Hound of Heaven in our stress
because I want to die
writing Haiku
or, better,
long lines, clean and syllabic as knotted bamboo. Yes!

1962

Spots of Blood

I am wearing absent-minded red
slippers and a red vest—
spots of blood
to match the broken English
of Count Dracula being interviewed
on the radio in the morning sun.
I touch the holes in my throat
where the poppies bud—spots of blood
spots of womantime. '14,000 rats',
Dracula is saying, and the interviewer
echoes, '14,000 rats! So beautiful',
he sighs, 'The Carpathian Mountains—
the photography, so seductive!' The Count
also loves the film; he has already seen it
several times. He tells in his dreamy voice
how he didn't need direction, didn't want
makeup, how he could have done it with his own
teeth. He glided in and out of this role
believing in reincarnation, in metamorphosis.
Yet 14,000 rats and the beleaguered
citizens of the Dutch town where those scenes
were shot (without him) are of no interest.
'And Hollywood?' the interviewer asks, himself
an actor, 'Hollywood next?' Who knows?
Who knows?

The blood pounds at my temples.
The women of the world parade before me
in red slippers and red vests, back and
forth, back and forth, fists clenched.
My heart emerges from my breast for
14,000 rats and the citizens of Delft,
for the women of the world in their menses.

Yet I too imitate a crime of passion:
Look at these hands. Look at the hectic
red painting my cheekbones as I metamorphose
in and out of the Buddha's eye, the *animus
mundi*.

In the morning sun Count Dracula leans

against my throat with his own teeth.
Breathing poppies. Thinking.

1980

Eschatology of Spring

Death, Judgement, Heaven, Hell,
and Spring. The Five Last Things,
the least of which I am, being in
the azaleas and dog-toothed violets
of the South of Canada. Do not tell me
this is a cold country. I am also in
the camellias and camas of early, of
abrupt birth.
We are shooting up for the bloody
judgement of the six o'clock news.
Quick, cut us out from the deadlines
of rotting newspapers, quick, for the
tiny skeletons and bulbs will tell you
how death grows and grows in Chile and
Chad. Quick, for the small bones pinch
me and insects divulge occult excrement
in the service of my hyacinth, my trailing
begonia. And if you catch me resting
beside the stream, sighing against
the headlines of this pastoral, take
up your gun, the flowers blossoming
from its barrel, and join this grief, this
grief: that there are lambs, elegant black-
footed lambs in this island's eschatology.
Beloved.

1980

The Days of the Unicorns

I remember when the unicorns
roved in herds through the meadow
behind the cabin, and how they would
lately pause, tilting their jewelled

horns to the falling sun as we shared
the tensions of private property
and the need to be alone.

Or as we walked along the beach
a solitary delicate beast
might follow on his soft paws
until we turned and spoke the words
to console him.

It seemed they were always near
ready to show their eyes and stare
us down, standing in their creamy
skins, pink tongues out
for our benevolence.

As if they knew that always beyond
and beyond the ladies were weaving them
into their spider looms.

I knew where they slept
and how the grass was bent
by their own wilderness
and I pitied them.

It was only yesterday, or seems
like only yesterday when we could
touch and turn and they came
perfectly real into our fictions.
But they moved on with the courtly sun
grazing peacefully beyond the story
horns lowering and lifting and
lowering.

I know this is scarcely credible now
as we cabin ourselves in cold
and the motions of panic
and our cells destroy each other
performing music and extinction
and the great dreams pass on
to the common good.

1980

From *Water and Light: Ghazals and Anti Ghazals*

The flow, flux, even the effluent stormy
in high wind, dashing into the poison mind.

Trees downed by a gale. Seawrack matting
the shore, the morning after. The wind said,

Take that, and that! and that! continuing
on its path with the same message for in-landers stranded.

Pathetic fallacies deep in these bones.
Pathetic oneness with weathers and cosmic dust.

Pretty pebble, divine bird, honorable tree—
all in me. Take this, and this, and this—in memory of.

*   *   *

My loves are dying. Or is it that my love
is dying, day by day, brief life, brief candle,

a flame, *flambeau*, torch, alive, singing
somewhere in the shadow: Here, this way, here.

Hear the atoms ambling, the genes a-tick
in grandfather's clock, in the old bones of beach.

Sun on the Sunday water in November.
Dead leaves on wet ground. The ferry leaves on time.

Time in your flight—O—a wristwatch strapped
to my heart, ticking erratically, winding down.

*   *   *

The pull, this way and that, ultimately into the pull
of the pen across the page.

Sniffing for poems, the forward memory
of hand beyond the grasp.

Not grasping, not at all. *Reaching* is
different—can't touch that sun.

Too hot. That star. This cross-eyed
vision. Days and nights, sun, moon—the up-there claptrap.

And down here, trappings of 'as above'—crosswalks,
traffic lights, sirens, this alexandrite burning on this hand.

*   *   *

Tuned lyre (lyrebird, mynah,
parrot, parakeet, peacock) paradox—

not musical, though the brilliant plumage
variegated for those who do not

sing well, screech, shriek, scream
in the jungle trees—the 'EE' sounds

unlyrical plumage, especially with 's'es.
On the other hand (plucked), sea, see,

or me, thee, three in the thicket,
perfectly musical

and coloured enough, though featherless,
for a kind of flying.

1984

ADELE WISEMAN
b. 1928

Ascent

Ascent is sheer delight,
but sudden birds must face
a danger of return
so swift it baffles flight.
And there, you'd think,
is where the skill comes in
to brake the dive,
but neither reflexes
nor timing can control
the throttle grip

of your hand on my heart
or my tailspin.
The perilous moment
for all high flyers
is the descent.

1982

Roofers

From my secluded porch
an angled glance away
There on the neighbour's roof
the brazen, agile youths
stripped to their honey skin
are hammering the air.

They bang my eyes awake
to swarm with covert care
and even less discretion
than their swagger knows,
the faint soft rolling bulge
where each young paunch begins.

Their sun-baked sweat-smooth glow
sends a kindling message
from high amoral sun
through my collector eyes,
sweetgrass smoke in mouth and thighs.

I would have just such coarse
such honeyed youths to roof
my grave impersonal
when I relinquish you,
that hammering to wake
the covert eye of dead
desire another stage
when I'm no longer there,
make something new to grow.

1986

Spaces

It's not the words the danger's in, it's in
the drops between, it's in the spaces of the dream
we fall, the danger's in the print, the way we trust
ourselves to structures on the page, believe
in guy wires taut with rhythms caught, safe nets
of springing rhyme. What mind's short reach can long
hold swinging words, hold slippery thought?
In the recurring dream the child's alone
high on suspended footbridge to the city park.
Spaces gape between collapsing boards,
the cataract's below, she clings to swinging ropes,
and mummy and the sandwiches are gone
and Tarzan's busy elsewhere saving Jane.
Write how mum held your forehead as you puked
out of the window of the old streetcar. Write
of the park the zoo the elms the feasts laid on
the living green. Write how you later missed
the sturdy bridge now concrete low on sluggish stream
and write how terror gathers in the spaces
and the fall is a recurring dream.

1986

JAY MACPHERSON
b. 1931

The Third Eye

Of three eyes, I would still give two for one.
The third eye clouds: its light is nearly gone.
The two saw green, saw sky, saw people pass:
The third eye saw through order like a glass
To concentrate, refine and rarify
And make a Cosmos of miscellany.
Sight, world and all to save alive that one
Fading so fast! Ah love, its light is done.

1957

Eve in Reflection

Painful and brief the act. Eve on the barren shore
Sees every cherished feature, plumed tree, bright grass,
Fresh spring, the beasts as placid as before
Beneath the inviolable glass.

There the lost girl gone under sea
Tends her undying grove, never raising her eyes
To where on the salt shell beach in reverie
The mother of all living lies.

The beloved face is lost from sight,
Marred in a whelming tide of blood:
And Adam walks in the cold night
Wilderness, waste wood.

1957

The Boatman

You might suppose it easy
For a maker not too lazy
To convert the gentle reader to an Ark:
But it takes a willing pupil
To admit both gnat and camel
—Quite an eyeful, all the crew that must embark.

After me when comes the deluge
And you're looking round for refuge
From God's anger pouring down in gush and spout,
Then you take the tender creature
—You remember, that's the reader—
And you pull him through his navel inside out.

That's to get his beasts outside him,
For they've got to come aboard him,
As the best directions have it, two by two.
When you've taken all their tickets
And you've marched them through his sockets,
Let the tempest bust Creation: heed not you.

For you're riding high and mighty
In a gale that's pushing ninety
With a solid bottom under you—that's his.
Fellow flesh affords a rampart,
And you've got along for comfort
All the world there ever shall be, was, and is.

1957

The Fisherman

The world was first a private park
Until the angel, after dark,
Scattered afar to wests and easts
The lovers and the friendly beasts.

And later still a home-made boat
Contained Creation set afloat,
No rift nor leak that might betray
The creatures to a hostile day.

But now beside the midnight lake
One single fisher sits awake
And casts and fights and hauls to land
A myriad forms upon the sand.

Old Adam on the naming-day
Blessed each and let it slip away:
The fisher of the fallen mind
Sees no occasion to be kind,

But on his catch proceeds to sup;
Then bends, and at one slurp sucks up
The lake and all that therein is
To slake that hungry gut of his,

Then whistling makes for home and bed
As the last morning breaks in red;
But God the Lord with patient grin
Lets down his hook and hoicks him in.

1957

The Anagogic Man

Noah walks with head bent down;
For between his nape and crown
He carries, balancing with care,
A golden bubble round and rare.

Its gently shimmering sides surround
All us and our worlds, and bound
Art and life, and wit and sense,
Innocence and experience.

Forbear to startle him, lest some
Poor soul to its destruction come,
Slipped out of mind and past recall
As if it never was at all.

O you that pass, if still he seems
One absent-minded or in dreams,
Consider that your senses keep
A death far deeper than his sleep.

Angel, declare: what sways when Noah nods?
The sun, the stars, the figures of the gods.

1957

Eurynome

Come all old maids that are squeamish
And afraid to make mistakes,
Don't clutter your lives up with boyfriends:
The nicest girls marry snakes.

If you don't mind slime on your pillow
And caresses as gliding as ice
—Cold skin, warm heart, remember,
And besides, they keep down the mice—

If you're really serious-minded,
It's the best advice you can take:

No rumpling, no sweating, no nonsense,
Oh who would not sleep with a snake?

1957

The Beauty of Job's Daughters

The old, the mad, the blind have fairest daughters.
Take Job: the beasts the accuser sends at evening
Shoulder his house and shake it; he's not there,
Attained in age to inwardness of daughters,
In all the land no women found so fair.

Angels and sons of God are nearest neighbours,
And even the accuser may repair
To walk with Job in pleasures of his daughters:
Wide shining rooms more warmly lit at evening,
Gardens beyond whose secrets scent the air.

Not wiles of men nor envy of the neighbours,
Riches of earth, nor what heaven holds more rare,
Can take from Job the beauty of his daughters,
The gardens in the rock, music at evening,
And cup so full that all who come must share.

Perhaps we passed them? it was late, or evening,
And surely those were desert stumps, not daughters,
In fact we doubt that they were ever there.
The old, the mad, the blind have fairest daughters.
In all the land no women found so fair.

1968

A Lost Soul

Some are plain lucky—we ourselves among them:
Houses with books, with gardens, all we wanted,
Work we enjoy, with colleagues we feel close to—
        Love we have, even:

True love and candid, faithful, strong as gospel,
Patient, untiring, fond when we are fretful.

Having so much, how is it that we ache for
　　　Those darker others?

Some days for them we could let slip the whole damn
Soft bed we've made ourselves, our friends in Heaven
Let slip away, buy back with blood our ancient
　　　Vampires and demons.

First loves and oldest, what names shall I call you?
Older to me than language, old as breathing,
Born with me, in this flesh: by now I know you're
　　　Greed, pride and envy.

Too long I've shut you out, denied acquaintance,
Favoured less barefaced vices, hoped to pass for
Reasonable, rate with those who more inclined to
　　　Self-hurt than murder.

You were my soul: in arrogance I banned you.
Now I recant—return, possess me, take my
Hands, bind my eyes, infallibly restore my
　　　Share in perdition.

1974

JOY KOGAWA
b. 1935

Ancestors' Graves in Kurakawa

Down down across the open sea to Shikoku
To story book island of mist and mystery
By train and bus through remote mountain villages
Following my father's boyhood backwards
Retracing the mountain path he crossed on rice husk slippers
With his dreams of countries beyond seas beyond seas
His dreams still intact, his flight perpetual
Back down the steep red mountain path
To the high hillside grave of my ancestors
Grey and green ferns hang down
Edging my faint beginnings with shades
Maintaining muteness in a wordless flickering

The hiddenness stretches beyond my reach
Strange dew drops through cedar incense
And I greet the dead who smile through trees
Accepting the pebbles that melt through my eyes.

1974

Day of the Bride

The day of the bride dawns
Through layers of white plaster skin
And multi-sashed kimono
Head made huge by lacquered hair—
She is swept ashore in her glass bottle
White and tight as a folded paper message
Eyes hidden in a swirl of green boughs.
She moves like a mannequin
Manoeuvred by centuries of ceremony
Under the weight of speech and incantation
A wail of priests and watching families
Beside rows of low tables
With small triangles of paper
Congratulatory slits of squid and curls of seaweed.
Then kneeling at the bend of a fresh memory
She is discarded by her heavy day
And is plunged into the twentieth century
Tiny apartment daily stream
As a barely visible
Folded paper speck

1974

Hangnail

Wondering about the importance of this hangnail
And its power over this massive hulk
Which dangles tenuously from its ledge
And this shuffling mass of a hangnail
From which the universe protrudes—
A hug might help
But I can't feel any cosmic arms
Nor earthly ones—

While walking I stepped on a giant moth
And in the long moment of its dying
All the accumulated injustices
Of squashed and battered bugs
Sacrificed on windshields
And sprayed to oblivion
Poured out of its eloquent wings
In one long fluttering—
And now the blood throbs in my thumb—
Attempting to atone the foot's misadventure?
Offering a salve of forgetfulness
To assuage my guilt?
An eye for an apple, a tooth for a pick
Kill the bugs if they make you sick—
The hangnail drones on interpreting itself
In the maze of my notions of justice
Which hang on as tenaciously and irritatingly
As a hangnail thread.

1974

If Your Mirror Breaks

If when you are holding a
hand mirror while sitting
in the front seat of a car
and the mirror breaks
you must stop everything quickly
step on the brakes
leap from the car.

If when you are holding in
your arms a mirror and you
feel the glass sudden in your veins—
if your throat bleeds with
brittle words and
you hear in the distance the
ambulance siren—

If your mirror breaks into
a tittering sound of tinkling glass
and you see the highway stretch

into a million staring splinters
you must stop everything gently
wait for seven long years
under a sky of whirling wheels

If your mirror breaks
oh if your mirror breaks—

1985

PAT LOWTHER
1935–1975

Leaning From City Window

Leaning from city window
absorbing heavy October sunset, clouds apricot and wool,
leaning far out to grasp traffic lights, cars and substantial people
(a Diesel truck bruises my heart in passing)
leaning far out, far out, till the wind is an arm at my back,
is a paratrooper sergeant.   I'm out!
See how the pavement receives me, shatters me,
see all my life spread in glittering shards on the cool cement,
glittering fragments of traffic lights, of sunset reflect.
Now the girls from the factory grind me beneath their sharp heels.
I am a sparkle of powdered glass on the sidewalk,
a smear of frost. Now a boy scuffs his toe and whirls me to air.
I am frost crystals, separate and dazzling.
I disseminate, claim all the city for my various estate.
Bidding myself farewell, I ride a stenographer's eyelash,
enter the open collar of a labourer's coat
and nest in the warm mat of hair at the base of his throat
and carousing above the street
ride like a carnival the wild loops of light in a neon sign.

1968

A Stone Diary

At the beginning I noticed
the huge stones on my path
I knew instinctively

why they were there
breathing as naturally
as animals
I moved them to ritual patterns
I abraded my hands
and made blood prints

Last week I became
aware of details
cubes of fool's gold
green and blue copper
crystal formations
fossils   shell casts
iron roses   candied gems

I thought of
the Empress Josephine,
the Burning of Troy
between her breasts,
of Ivan the Terrible lecturing
on the virtues of rubies.
They were dilettantes.

By the turn of the week
I was madly in love
with stone. Do you know
how beautiful it is
to embrace stone
to curve all your body
against its surfaces?

Yesterday I began
seeing you as
desirable as a stone
I imagined you coming
onto the path with me
even your mouth
a carved stone

Today for the first time
I noticed how coarse
my skin has grown
but the stones shine

with their own light,
they grow smoother
and smoother

1977

Octopus

The octopus is beautifully
functional as an umbrella;
at rest a bag of rucked skin
sags like an empty scrotum
his jelled eyes sad and bored

but taking flight: look
how lovely purposeful
in every part:
the jet vent smooth
as modern plumbing
the webbed pinwheel of tentacles
moving in perfect accord
like a machine dreamed
by Leonardo

1977

Coast Range

Just north of town
the mountains start to talk
back-of-the-head buzz
of high stubbled meadows
minute flowers
moss gravel and clouds

They're not snobs, these mountains,
they don't speak Rosicrucian,
they sputter with
billygoat-bearded creeks
bumsliding down
to splat into the sea

they talk with the casual
tongues of water
rising in trees

They're so humble they'll let you
blast highways through them
baring their iron and granite
sunset-coloured bones
broken for miles

And nights when
clouds foam on a beach
of clear night sky,
those high slopes creak
in companionable sleep

        *   *   *

Move through gray green
aurora of rain
to the bare fact:
The land is bare.

Even the curly opaque Pacific
forest, chilling you full awake
with wet branch-slaps,
is somehow bare
stainless as sunlight:

The land is what's left
after the failure
of every kind of metaphor.

        *   *   *

The plainness of first things
trees
gravel
rocks
naive root atom
of philosophy's first molecule

The mountains reject nothing
but can crack

open your mind
just by being intractably there

Atom: that which can not
be reduced

You can gut them
blast them
to slag
the shapes they've made in the sky
cannot be reduced

1977

Anniversary Letter to Pablo

That first time
on the moongravel
they jumped like clumsy fawns.
They were drunk in love
with their own history;
Satori flash lighted
their indelible footprints.

But you warmed the moon
in a loving cup,
in the thawing
water of your eyes,
you the man who moves
under the hill,
the man who kisses stone.

Custodians of footsteps
and magnets,
you take mineral glitter
in the cup
of your hand,
it becomes veins.
You own also the moon
now where they touched.

1977

CLAIRE HARRIS
b. 1937

Black Sisyphus

To propitiate the dreaming god at his centre
for months my father drove down green uneven

roads to the capital where tar flowed under
noonday heat in daily manouevres around new obstacles

to take form again in cold pale morning
he drove those roads in mutters searching through

the crumpled pathways of his brain while his
voice rose and stumbled in the sibilant argument

he enjoyed with life   he could not be
convinced that being human was not enough

that there was no bridge he could cross
he would not 'forget de man' nor 'leave

him to God'   these were his sky/trees/
his streets to name   was he not greeted

by all he passed   naming   from a wilderness
of loss his fathers created this island garden

he would not be cast out again   he
rode his right to words   pointed and named

the road from one way of life to another is hard
*those who are ahead have a long way to go**

missionary zeal could not stomach such clarity
they damned him   thundered fire   brimstone   the sin

of pride   thus my father and his letters
raced weekly to the centre   the apology

*Transtromer, 'From an African Diary' (1963)

won   he stood   nodded   bowed   strode in his own
echoing silence   out of lowered eyes/bells/incense

the worn organ's cough   out of village voices
wheeling in cracked Kyries

to stand on the church steps muttering:
it is enough to be a man   today

his fingers kneading my six year old hands
as if they would refashion them

1986

Framed

She is in your painting   the one you bought when the taxi
snarled in market lines   you jumped out and grabbed
a picture of stilted wooden houses against the vivid island
even then there was recognition

She is the woman in a broken pair of men's shoes   her
flesh slipped down like old socks around her ankles   a tray
of laundry on her head   I am there too   but I would not
be like her   at supper she set the one plate and the whole
cup at my place   for herself a mug a bowl my leavings
they said I resembled her   I spent hours before the mirror
training my mouth to different lines

At night while I read   she folded the blanket on her
narrow board   coalfire smooth on her face   she boiled
scrubbed   ironed   musk of soap and others soil like
mist around her head   often she dreamed   I would have
a maid   like her   she laughed   I studied harder harder
she grieved   I was grown a woman   I was grown
without affinity

For the calling   her eroded hands   cupped like a chalice
she offered me the blasted world as if to say   this is our
sacrament   drink   I would not   this is all there is   I
could not   I left school   I left   she faded
the island faded   styles changed   you hid the dusty
painting in the attic   But I am still there   the one in

middle ground   my face bruising lines of soft white
sheets   my hand raised as if to push against the frame

1986

Variations: One

A (ME): of very limited or narrow outlook or scope

As this wind enters the eucalyptus
so would I enter you   in light
strokings   small rufflings   the light shedding
from me to gather in your trunk and stems

I now green as your leaves

You and I would shudder and rasp   flutter
and tap hollow trunks together
so we would work in us   then leave

Only that you and I would excel us

See how the eucalyptus glints taller
the wind gathers strength
beyond the river

Variations: Two

V (O) FR: to limit or bound in respect of space.

After rain light falls across bowls of fruit on the table
startling the apples the green and yellow oranges into clarity
they become the essence of orange of apple
you stand on this using it as your metaphor
saying   choose
I have never understood why I should
the delicate pink and white of apple blossoms
or the sharp citrus tang of orange trees
I want them both in different seasons
as I want you sprawled across the bed taking up
your half and mine on some days
the clever geometric sheets incredibly undone
your knee at my back

But there are days I make my bed
with drifts of snow or apple blossoms
and want to lie in it alone enjoying the expansive calm
the different silences

Variations: Three

A (ME): not subject to or susceptible to change

Once in the rain you took off your coat
wrapped it around the statue of the dead
beats in the children's park
as if you meant it

            and I loved you

Today there is this brief old man who
lifts his courtly hat and bows
to the bag-lady muttering at folded bits
on the park bench
as if she is

            and I love you

1986

The Web

Today the world's strong breath dawns silver on Lanzarote
tints flurries of leaves surging across black lava lawns
silvers the torn froth of clouds   suffuses a sky given
pale to smooth pale sea   there it curves beyond
to where another earth lies in darkness

The moon in its first quarter ghosts gently towards
the west   in the east a delicate luminous opening
all this invests the too early bulldozers   the trucks
grumbling in gravel   the cranes and concrete villas
rising against the surf   helmeted workmen intent on
beating the heat   take this silver breath   this numinous
dawn as their right   they breathe it in and it comes

back blue and fiery   and quick   they know how well it
gleams around their squat white houses   hugs the natural
cruelties as a pearl its heart

So does Cat know hurtling through it   mine
is the stranger's surprise and delight   the shock
of recognition one hears so much about   suddenly what
is and is not slips by   and does not   for one heart beat
i am cat's leap   against my stilled hibiscus red i am
crane's pause   wave's warm tongue   i am boots and
the crouched woman's scream   then the flow resumes

1986

And So . . . Home

I walk the raw paths through winds that crowd me
now this autumn comes around before I'm ready
pulls at my slack time tautening
for a moment no existence at all

Behind the grave apartment towers clouds
pile up   rattle spare bones of rain   leaves
lift and twirl   among all that gold
the air is winged   crackling

Why now her song surprises me I'm not sure
memory spills from my lips   ribbons
crisp satin ribbons   grosgrain   so long ago

My mother   her fingers part my hair make
four neat plaits that dovetail on each side
become one that is crossed and pinned

She holds out a rainbow of ribbons says
choose one   ribbons hanging from her fingers
like paths   how can I choose when any choice
means a giving up   years later shucking the island

As painful as shucking skin   yet I left
weaving a new space to trap the voice
I thought I could   must return   my navel string

Buried where the rich fantasy   of peoples
stranded by empire jostled on those stunned hummocks
history's low road under the bruising sun

Now loving this chill autumn rain I know it has been too long
a memory of dark hands intelligent with a child's
ribbons   hands vulnerable among ruins
something to conjure with

1986

LOLA LEMIRE TOSTEVIN
b. 1937

From *'Sophie*

*

I write because I can't sing   I am the book exiled
from my voice in search of a melody but like the woman
who is blind because her eyes are filled with seeing
and like the woman who is deaf because her ears are
filled with hearing I am mute because my voice is filled
with words and unlike music I can only be understood
and not heard

As *These Our Mothers* have said we cannot hide
from ourselves the fictional character of the first A
but neither can I hide the love and the endurance
of that fiction   I write the letter *a* as my ancestral
cry   cry of the *anima*   a vociferous bird from Patagonia
whose beak is a remedy for those whose words fall out
of their mouth too early or too late

I echo the bird's song with eloquence   oracular mood
of the loon   invent music to the measure of its breath
but because I am word it will never be heard

*

harmony doesn't exist before the lyre
the village wizard said as she placed

seven pebbles

on my tongue and sealed my mouth
with moss from a dead woman's skull

anointed me with weapon salve
to cure the wound through that which caused it

seventh daughter of a seventh daughter
she understood the ancient art of alchemy

that extracts from stones a substance
reducible to its most perfect form

seven letters

that put to the mouth the sounding
and O how that sound surrenders

/

once the word was invented it was just a matter of
time before we all set out to find the real thing
and like the omnipotent being that brings itself into
existence you walked in   stood your post   ceased to be
a figment of my imagination

what did you change from?   which game?   whose power
of enchantment grew out of whose chimera?

your lion's head
the body of a goat
a dragon's tail
your face a fable

your phrases tracing shackles around my thin shin bones

when it's a matter of getting to the point   to the
source you outrun me curious courser swift as the
arrow you follow while I crawl at the tortuous pace
of the crooked foot tortoise in search of the sound
your arrow makes when it reaches then wrenches from
the real thing

/

when a body attracts a body with a force
proportional to the distance that exists
between them the laws that govern their fall
are even more beautiful and intricate
than the stars above

> *pi* in the sky

and bodies as obedient as any other
to the laws of gravitation tilt
a few degrees to the west

> wobble

are lost forever since the earth
slipped a little
as we fell

/

a woman having a drink late at night   wonders
what he's up to and if given the same event
in a different part of the country could the two
not be happening at the same time?   she wonders
how common sense has come to think of itself as
a little rum   a little *nachtmusik*   and small gestures
that persist through space and time

she knows she shouldn't be doing this

she should be writing a poem in which she situates herself
in terms of a desire that passes on through writing
but each time she begins to write she feels she has to reinvent
the world   and even old Archimedes given a lever and a fixed
point only had to move it a few inches   she wonders

how she came to this place between writing as body
and writing as erasure of the body   she wonders
if passivity and passion stem from the same root

she follows the imaginary path of a gesture
that promises to recite their archaic history

the way an extinct animal is reconstructed
from the single facet of a bone

/

the floor around my desk is littered with books   crumpled
papers   all the tools necessary to the engineering of poems
scales   ruler   a magic square   an artesian well   a compass
that keeps pivoting north   a rhomboid. . . . the poem wants
precision   the exact properties and relations of angles
and lines   craves perfection the way a dog is perfected
by the huntsman's art

an oldie on a radio queries softly '. . . how deep is the ocean
how high is the sky . . .' inconceivable notions of depth and
height   fables of landscape

it was for purely aesthetic reasons one philosopher wanted
the earth round   and because the moon shines by reflected
light they came to the theory of eclipse   someone must have
stood in a candle lit room   covered one eye and moved a
marble back and forth between the other eye and the night
the outer ring of the moon visible around the marble
small ivory lunules on all sides   the boundary between light
and dark never sharp

1988

MARGARET ATWOOD
b. 1939

Death of a Young Son By Drowning

He, who navigated with success
the dangerous river of his own birth
once more set forth

on a voyage of discovery
into the land I floated on
but could not touch to claim.

His feet slid on the bank,
the currents took him;
he swirled with ice and trees in the swollen water

and plunged into distant regions,
his head a bathysphere;
through his eyes' thin glass bubbles

he looked out, reckless adventurer
on a landscape stranger than Uranus
we have all been to and some remember.

There was an accident; the air locked,
he was hung in the river like a heart.
They retrieved the swamped body,

cairn of my plans and future charts,
with poles and hooks
from among the nudging logs.

It was spring, the sun kept shining, the new grass
lept to solidity;
my hands glistened with details.

After the long trip I was tired of waves.
My foot hit rock. The dreamed sails
collapsed, ragged.

> I planted him in this country
> like a flag.

1970

There Is Only One of Everything

Not a tree but the tree
we saw, it will never exist, split by the wind
                    and bending down
like that again. What will push out of the earth

later, making it summer, will not be
grass, leaves, repetition, there will
have to be other words. When my

eyes close language vanishes. The cat
with the divided face, half black half orange
nests in my scruffy fur coat, I drink tea,

fingers curved around the cup, impossible
to duplicate these flavours. The table
and freak plates glow softly, consuming themselves,

I look out at you and you occur
in this winter kitchen, random as trees or sentences,
entering me, fading like them, in time you will disappear

but the way you dance by yourself
on the tile floor to a worn song, flat and mournful,
so delighted, spoon waved in one hand, wisps of
                              roughened hair

sticking up from your head, it's your surprised
body, pleasure I like. I can even say it,
though only once and it won't

last: I want this. I want
this.

1974

You Begin

You begin this way:
this is your hand,
this is your eye,
that is a fish, blue and flat
on the paper, almost
the shape of an eye.
This is your mouth, this is an O
or a moon, whichever
you like. This is yellow.

Outside the window
is the rain, green
because it is summer, and beyond that
the trees and then the world,

which is round and has only
the colours of these nine crayons.

This is the world, which is fuller
and more difficult to learn than I have said.
You are right to smudge it that way
with the red and then
the orange: the world burns.

Once you have learned these words
you will learn that there are more
words than you can ever learn.
The word *hand* floats above your hand
like a small cloud over a lake.
The word *hand* anchors
your hand to this table,
your hand is a warm stone
I hold between two words.

This is your hand, these are my hands, this is the world,
which is round but not flat and has more colours
than we can see.

It begins, it has an end,
this is what you will
come back to, this is your hand.

1978

The Woman Who Could Not Live
With Her Faulty Heart

I do not mean the symbol
of love, a candy shape
to decorate cakes with,
the heart that is supposed
to belong or break;

I mean this lump of muscle
that contracts like a flayed biceps,
purple-blue, with its skin of suet,
its skin of gristle, this isolate,
this caved hermit, unshelled

turtle, this one lungful of blood,
no happy plateful.

All hearts float in their own
deep oceans of no light,
wetblack and glimmering,
their four mouths gulping like fish.
Hearts are said to pound:
this is to be expected, the heart's
regular struggle against being drowned.

But most hearts say, I want, I want,
I want, I want. My heart
is more duplicitous,
though no twin as I once thought.
It says, I want, I don't want, I
want, and then a pause.
It forces me to listen,

and at night it is the infra-red
third eye that remains open
while the other two are sleeping
but refuses to say what it has seen.

It is a constant pestering
in my ears, a caught moth, limping drum,
a child's fist beating
itself against the bedsprings:
on breathless nights,
a desolate white memento.

Or: these are the lost children,
those who have died or thickened
to full growth and gone away.

The dolls are their souls or cast skins
which line the shelves of our bedrooms
and museums, disguised as outmoded toys,
images of our sorrow,
shedding around themselves
five inches of limbo.

1978

Notes Towards a Poem
That Can Never Be Written

For Carolyn Forché

i
This is the place
you would rather not know about,
this is the place that will inhabit you,
this is the place you cannot imagine,
this is the place that will finally defeat you

where the word *why* shrivels and empties
itself. This is famine.

ii
There is no poem you can write
about it, the sandpits
where so many were buried
& unearthed, the unendurable
pain still traced on their skins.

This did not happen last year
or forty years ago but last week.
This has been happening,
this happens.

We make wreaths of adjectives for them,
we count them like beads,
we turn them into statistics & litanies
and into poems like this one.

Nothing works.
They remain what they are.

iii
The woman lies on the wet cement floor
under the unending light,
needle marks on her arms put there
to kill the brain
and wonders why she is dying.

She is dying because she said.
She is dying for the sake of the word.
It is her body, silent
and fingerless, writing this poem.

iv
It resembles an operation
but it is not one

nor despite the spread legs, grunts
& blood, is it a birth.

Partly it's a job,
partly it's a display of skill
like a concerto.

It can be done badly
or well, they tell themselves.

Partly it's an art.

v
The facts of this world seen clearly
are seen through tears;
why tell me then
there is something wrong with my eyes?

To see clearly and without flinching,
without turning away,
this is agony, the eyes taped open
two inches from the sun.

What is it you see then?
Is it a bad dream, a hallucination?
Is it a vision?
What is it you hear?

The razor across the eyeball
is a detail from an old film.
It is also a truth.
Witness is what you must bear.

vi
In this country you can say what you like
because no one will listen to you anyway,
it's safe enough, in this country you can try to write
the poem that can never be written,
the poem that invents
nothing and excuses nothing,
because you invent and excuse yourself each day.

Elsewhere, this poem is not invention.
Elsewhere, this poem takes courage.
Elsewhere, this poem must be written
because the poets are already dead.

Elsewhere, this poem must be written
as if you are already dead,
as if nothing more can be done
or said to save you.

Elsewhere you must write this poem
because there is nothing more to do.

1981

Earth

It isn't winter that brings it
out, my cowardice,
but the thickening summer I wallow in
right now, stinking of lilacs, green
with worms & stamens duplicating themselves
each one the same

I squat among rows of seeds & impostors
and snout my hand into the juicy dirt:
charred chicken bones, rusted nails,
dogbones, stones, stove ashes.
Down there is another hand, yours, hopeless,
down there is a future.

in which you're a white white picture
with a name I forgot to write
underneath, and no date,

in which you're a suit
hanging with its stubs of sleeves
in a cupboard in a house
in a city I've never entered,

a missed beat in space
which nevertheless unrolls itself
as usual. As usual:
that's why I don't want to go on with this.

(I'll want to make a hole in the earth
the size of an implosion, a leaf, a dwarf
star, a cave
in time that opens back & back into
absolute darkness and at last
into a small pale moon of light
the size of a hand,
I'll want to call you out of the grave
in the form of anything at all)

1981

Nothing

Nothing like love to put blood
back in the language,
the difference between the beach and its
discrete rocks & shards, a hard
cuneiform, and the tender cursive
of waves; bone & liquid fishegg, desert
& saltmarsh, a green push
out of death. The vowels plump
again like lips or soaked fingers, and the fingers
themselves move around these
softening pebbles as around skin. The sky's
not vacant and over there but close
against your eyes, molten, so near
you can taste it. It tastes of

salt. What touches
you is what you touch.

1981

GWENDOLYN MacEWEN
1941–1987

A Breakfast for Barbarians

my friends, my sweet barbarians,
there is that hunger which is not for food—
but an eye at the navel turns the appetite
round
with visions of some fabulous sandwich,
the brain's golden breakfast
                                eaten with beasts
                                with books on plates

let us make an anthology of recipes,
let us edit for breakfast
our most unspeakable appetites—
let us pool spoons, knives
and all cutlery in a cosmic cuisine,
let us answer hunger
with boiled chimera
and apocalyptic tea,
an arcane salad of spiced bibles,
tossed dictionaries—
                        (O my barbarians
                        we will consume our mysteries)

and can we, can we slake the gaping eye of our desires?
we will sit around our hewn wood table
until our hair is long and our eyes are feeble,
eating, my people, O my insatiates,
eating until we are no more able
to jack up the jaws any longer—

to no more complain of the soul's vulgar cavities,
to gaze at each other over the rust-heap of cutlery,
drinking a coffee that takes an eternity—
till, bursting, bleary,

we laugh, barbarians, and rock the universe—
and exclaim to each other over the table
over the table of bones and scrap metal
over the gigantic junk-heaped table:

by God that was a meal

1968

The Discovery

do not imagine that the exploration
ends, that she has yielded all her mystery
or that the map you hold
cancels further discovery

I tell you her uncovering takes years
takes centuries, and when you find her naked
look again,
admit there is something else you cannot name,
a veil, a coating just above the flesh
which you cannot remove by your mere wish

when you see the land naked, look again
(burn your maps, that is not what I mean),
I mean the moment when it seems most plain
is the moment when you must begin again

1969

Dark Pines Under Water

This land like a mirror turns you inward
And you become a forest in a furtive lake;
The dark pines of your mind reach downward,
You dream in the green of your time,
Your memory is a row of sinking pines.

Explorer, you tell yourself this is not what you came for
Although it is good here, and green;
You had meant to move with a kind of largeness,
You had planned a heavy grace, an anguished dream.

But the dark pines of your mind dip deeper
And you are sinking, sinking, sleeper
In an elementary world;
There is something down there and you want it told.

1969

From *The T.E. Lawrence Poems*

WATER

When you think of it, water is everything. Or rather,
Water ventures into everything and becomes everything.
      It has
All tastes and moods imaginable; water is history
And the end of the world is water also.
                          I have tasted water
From London to Miranshah. In France it tasted
Of Crusaders' breastplates, swords, and tunnels of rings
On ladies' fingers.
            In the springs of Lebanon water had
No color, and was therefore all colors,
                      outside of Damascus
It disguised itself as snow and let itself be chopped
And spooned onto the stunned red grapes of summer.

For years I have defended water, even though I am told
          there are other drinks.
Water will never lie to you, even when it insinuates itself
Into someone else's territory. Water has style.

Water has no conscience and no shame; water
          thrives on water, is self-quenching.
It often tastes of brine and ammonia, and always
Knows its way back home.

When you want to travel very far, do as the Bedouin do—
Drink to overflowing when you can,
                  and then
Go sparingly between wells.

1982

THE DESERT

Only God lives there in the seductive Nothing
That implodes into pure light. English makes Him
              an ugly monosyllable, but Allah breathes
A fiery music from His tongue, ignites the sands,
             invents a terrible love that is
The very name of pain.

The desert preserves Him
           as the prophets found Him, massive and alone.
They went there, into that awful Zero
                  to interpret Him,
       for Himself to know, for He said: Help me,
I am the One who is alone, not you. Tell Me who I am.

Camels lean into the desert, lost in some thought
          so profound it can only be guessed. When
Will God invent man?   When
            will the great dream end?
My skin crawls with a horrible beauty in this
         Nothingness, this Everything—

I fall to my knees in the deep white sand, and my head
        implodes into pure light.

1982

THE ABSOLUTE ROOM

We came to a place which was the center of ourselves
       in the desert between Aleppo and Hama;
We came to this Roman place where a hundred scents
       were built somehow right into the walls.
So the old man and the boy led us through courts
     of jasmine, and many other flowers, then

Into this great hall where all the scents slayed
     each other, and were still, and all
We breathed was pure desert air.

                 We call
this room the sweetest of them all,

You said.
> And I thought: *Because there is nothing here.*

I knew then that you possessed nothing of me, and I
> possessed nothing of you, Dahoum.
We were wealthy and stuffed with a wondrous nothing
> that filled the room and everything around.

You looked into my eyes, the windows to my soul,
> and said that because they were blue
You could see right through them, holes in my skull,
> to the quiet, powerful sky beyond.

1982

THUNDER-SONG

Two musicians played before the storm broke; one played
Wind-song, wind in the dry valley grass;
>   one played
>   dark, blind music on two strings. They both
Sang of war and love and death—what else is there
>   to sing for?

Then came the armies of rain, wave after wave of it,
And a murderous blue lightning which brought the stones
>   to life in the courtyard outside.
>   Two lions
>   on a pedestal laughed and laughed at us, with
>   blue rain slobbering down their jaws, and then

Came the god, striding along an inscription towards the door.

The first musician controlled the thunder with his pipe
And the second explored the spaces in between
>   the statements of the light.
>   In the place we were,
The place between twin rivers, Babylon, all was articulate
And utterly real,
>   Then the storm subsided and the pipe wept
At its passing. I knew that if ever I died it would be thus:

A helmeted seven-foot god coming quietly in blue light
Towards me.

1982

The Grand Dance

I promised I would never turn you into poetry, but
Allow this liar these wilful, wicked lines.

I am simply trying to track you down
In preworlds and afterworlds
And the present myriad inner worlds
Which whirl around in the carousel of space.

I hurl breathless poems against my lord Death,
Send these words, these words
Careening into the beautiful darkness.

And where do all the words go?
They say that somewhere out there in space
Every word uttered by every man
Since the beginning of man
Is still sounding. Afterthoughts,

Lethal gossip of the spheres.

Dance then, dance in the city streets,
Your body a fierce illusion of flesh, of energy,
The particles of light cast off from your hair
Illumine you for this moment only.

Your afterimage claims the air
And every moment is Apocalypse—

Avatar, deathless
Anarchy.

1987

The White Horse

This is the first horse to come into the world;
It heaved itself out of the sea to stand now
In a field of dizzy sunlight,
Its eyes huge with joy and wisdom,
Its head turned towards you, wondering
            why you are wondering

And how it comes about that you are here, when
Shrapnel from wars whose causes are forgotten
Has invaded the soft legs and bellies of children
And phosphorous bombs have made burnt ivory
            of the limbs of lovers
In Ireland and Lebanon and all the broken countries
Of the universe where this horse has never been.

You reach out your hand to touch it, and
This is the first time you have ever seen
            your hand, as it is also
The first time you have smelled the blue fire
Within a stone, or tasted blue air, or
Heard what the sea says when it talks in its sleep.

But hasn't the brilliant end come, you wonder,
And isn't the world still burning?

Go and tell this: It is morning,
And this horse with a mane the colour of seafoam
Is the first horse that the world has ever seen,
The white horse which stands now watching you
Across this field of endless sunlight.

1987

JENI COUZYN
b. 1942

From *Christmas In Africa*

I   IN THE HOUSE OF THE FATHER

Christmas, the turning time, the final reckoning and the
forgiveness, we rode towards each year, over humps of
bitterness, towards the father

omnipotent and bountiful night rider with his magical
reindeer and sack full of gifts—
you could rely on him always to be there when you got there

accept the culmination of your year in his lap
hear all, forgive with a wish, and let you
begin all over;

a time of reprieve and new resolutions, time when you could
believe in new beginnings, a time of peace and long
playtime. With a hand in the dark

it began before dawn. The sun would rise over the city
as we passed the last gold hills of the mine dumps. Always
I saw children leaping up them, and in my head, in golden depths

a heap of little skeletons. Then the long hot hours dreaming
through the dorps each its single tree and tin roofs blazing
each its lone dog barking and black silent men

propped on the verandah of the general store, drinking
lemonade. Endless car games, the singing game chanting every
      rhyme we knew
from ten green bottles to jesus loves me over the veld

to pass the time. At last, crossing, purple and lonely
the valley of a thousand hills, the tropical
deep smell of heavy flowers would glut the evening

and my father offered sixpence for the first to see the sea.
And there it was after a sudden unbending—that immense
      blue promise.
Then inland into the sugar cane in the deep of the night

the rustle of dunes and the sugar cane fields
the farmers who kept pythons fifty feet long to keep the rats down
and at midnight

the cottage. O the damp smell of foliage, smell of salt
and the sea's heavy breathing in the night, stray cries
of live things, batswing, shadows, sleep, and a ring of mornings.

The snakes were the price. In their hundreds they inhabited
our world at christmas. They were the hazard
in the garden. And they were everywhere

tangled in undergrowth, slithering over your feet in the pathway
stretched across doorways in the sun
lurking under the banana plant and nesting in the luckybean tree

they were everywhere, everywhere. And happiness was everywhere
in the father's time, who came down from heaven
in his red dressing gown and my father's shoes at the appointed
     time

cottonwool beard lopsided across his grin
his arms full of parcels.
His was the future that always came, keeping its promise.

In the house of the father the year would turn
a flower full blown, shedding its petals.
Glistened in your hand a free gift, a clean seed.

1975

House of Changes

My body is a wide house
a commune
of bickering women, hearing
their own breathing
denying each other.

Nearest the door
ready in her black leather
is *Vulnerable*. She lives in the hall
her face painted with care

her black boots reaching her crotch
her black hair shining
her skin milky and soft as butter.
If you should ring the doorbell
she would answer
and a wound would open across her eyes
as she touched your hand.

On the stairs, glossy and determined
is *Mindful*. She's the boss, handing out
punishments and rations and examination
papers with precise
justice. She keeps her perceptions in a huge
album under her arm
her debts in the garden with the weedkill
friends in a card-index
on the windowsill of the sittingroom
and a tape-recording of the world
on earphones
which she plays to herself over and over
assessing her life
writing summaries.

In the kitchen is *Commendable*.
The only lady in the house who
dresses in florals
she is always busy, always doing something
for someone she has
a lot of friends. Her hands are quick and
cunning as blackbirds
her pantry is stuffed with loaves and fishes
she knows the times of trains and
mends fuses and makes
a lot of noise with the vacuum cleaner.
In her linen cupboard, new-ironed and neatly
folded, she keeps her resentments like
wedding presents—each week
takes them out for counting not to
lose any but would never think of
using any being a lady.

Upstairs in a white room is
my favourite. She is *Equivocal*

has no flesh on her bones
that are changeable as yarrow stalks.
She hears her green plants talking
watches the bad dreams under the world
unfolding
spends all her days and nights
arranging her symbols
never sleeps
never eats hamburgers
never lets anyone into her room
never asks for anything.

In the basement is *Harmful*.
She is the keeper of weapons
the watchdog. Keeps intruders at bay
but the others keep her
locked up in the daytime and when she escapes
she comes out screaming
smoke streaming from her nostrils
flames on her tongue
razor-blades for fingernails
skewers for eyes.

I am *Imminent*
live out in the street
watching them. I lodge myself in other people's
heads with a sleeping bag
strapped to my back.
One day I'll perhaps get to like them enough
those rough, truthful women
to move in. One by one
I'm making friends with them all
unobtrusively, slow and steady
slow and steady.

1978

Cartography of the Subtle Heart

It has circles of light fragments
that shift endlessly, mandala
in a child's kaleidoscope.

It's roughly the size
of a human heart, centred in my chest exactly
as my heart is.

I am not taken in by that scarlet
harrowing the surgeons uncover.
I know the cavity they work in

from within my own body—
a vortex of hot winds
and bottomless dark. All my work

is to fill it with icons
shards of bright glass
in their desperate mosaic.

When my daughter
sprang from my body in her cocoon of light
trusting me utterly

it filled up with a syrup
warm and flowing but time
has returned it to crystals. I know it now

not as a wound that cripples
more than any other crippled person
lives in their damage

but as a doorway to the world
she came from, lianas of light around her
radiant and star-bright.

1985

GAIL FOX

b. 1942

Cartoons

What the poor devil
thought she was doing in
that nightmare

drawing pictures on her
wrists, the artistic
razor

doing such weird
cartoons of her husband
lover—

Listen, Michael,
I talked to her for
a while

because the lump of
leaving you was
too real

I tried to tell
her, 'don't do such
things to your

beautiful wrists,'
and she knew she
shouldn't

Then she drew some
pencil sketches of
caterpillars

and horses and the
ideal woman with
a mare's

head running through
her face—Michael
it was too late

for romance and
I left her almost
sobbing with

relief that she
had found me to
talk to

While I came
here to this half-lighted
room of

snoring loonies to
draw this poem
across the wrist

of my last touch
of your beautiful
hand

Do you know I
am an artist with
words?

That I want to
fuck the dictionary
or go blind

so that I can
forget the way things
look here

and only describe
them with symbols and
sounds?

That poor devil
with her talented
razor and eyes

looking everywhere
for the blood
under the bandages

And then me with
my black pen
writing

these idiotic
poems—what is
the sanity

that I find with
these crazy words
together

impossible symbols
to recommend your
whole beauty to me

The time of weeping
the time of dying,
the time of sleep

draws near—Michael,
I crawl from here
to a

very dark bedroom
without you, but
clutching this poem

about my life—
is that a kind of
slashing of the

wrists? Already
my hot blood rises,
Michael.

1976

Portrait

She slipped. Heels over head she landed
in a bucket of blue paint. Fluent as blue,
the day was green—magnificent. How
describe the green after an accident?

That's twice you've rescued me, she said,
bearing a resemblance to a shaky Rembrandt.
I dried her off and she broke into tears,
deftly combing strands of hair in place.

The other rescue was scientific. She
could only see people blurred, a distinction
allowed those with the green eyes of photo-
synthesis in their brains.

Trees also have this problem, I pointed
out, and she laughed hysterically, my sister,
while grandmother politely shuffled
cards and waited to deal them out.

Later I found such advice strangely terrible,
my cat suddenly malevolent around my
beautiful and suddenly ripped to pieces
skirt, my sister, crazy.

And all my teeth ground to little bits
in my pitch and feverish sleep; my sister,
my metaphor for intensity and parlour games,
smashed between two cars at midnight.

1980

DIANA HARTOG
b. 1942

Ode to Ontario

—So that I might praise a man newly weaned
from your bright smog, Ontario, one who burns
with the intensity of five steel mills
and has never given in to sanity or beauty,

but one who was constant in recording the geography
of your faults without drawing conclusions. This feat,
to love originally, requires of the brain
benign bruise spots and of the heart
a willingness to observe teeth-marks in the face of love

His face—with its parted hair and choir boy
smile above a perfectly-tied tie and with the basset hound
of Niagara falling all over his lap. Androgynous Ontario,
don't weep. You have lost an amorous poet
but everything to be said for British Columbia
is easily said—a lush whorl of fir compared
to your flat belly and the modest mound
of Mount Hope. Remember, he is almost forty
and you have been everything to him—chum,
lover, hag. He could see into your future
and saw himself there, beating you with a cane,
blaming you for your distance. Yes—

I have taken him in my arms, folded him within
new species of vegetation and mountains
he will never learn the names of.
He will never know me as he has known you, Ontario:
heading west towards the East, he wants secrets now
and throws himself on the ridge of my body
in vain, in successive waves of consciousness.

1983

Courtesy of Texaco

Life is nothing like opera—you meet a nice man
and then you never see him again.
Nothing like the radio on Saturday afternoons, when the Met's
red tonnage of curtain sweeps aside lint
and arias swoop cumulus: twin awnings pooled with rain
or the great ponderous breasts of women prone to diabetes.

But listen! Madame Butterfly is on her last pair of gloves: her cry
hurtles towards the fan on the bureau
where blades slice it scarlet, a smear
of ribbons fallen to the floor.

That was her *seppku* we heard. 'Seppku'—the Japanese diminutive
for Madame Butterfly's favorite niece, right?

—and not another failed attempt to align
knife and fork parallel to the universe. It's four, it's over,
time for tea. Beyond the sliding glass door and the rusting hibachi
the waves are behaving beautifully: calm, almost flat,
they deposit along the sand the foam that
gathers at the corners of the mouth when speaking in public.

Held up against the view and inspected for spots, a silver
                                  sugarspoon
moons the oblong moronic face one is issued at birth
if your mother wept too much (and you in utero, riding the swells)
or trusted the soothing gentle tone of the larger drug companies.

I'll admit, my preference is to be in the flesh in a darkening
opera house. But first a nice man
would have to shuffle sideways down the long row of knees
and ease without a word into the empty seat I'd saved by placing
a hand on the worn ruby velvet—to indicate I wasn't alone,
that someone would be joining me.

1986

The Future of Flight

Love's long bleached-blonde hair will always weep from a tower
as we pull out fistfuls, shinnying up.

For those of military bearing there's the ruse of the Cannon,
its cold muzzle raised at dawn to aim the soul's black dot.

More common is the Dream, in which flailing our arms
we lift off a few inches, skimming the lawn-chairs and zinnias.

Or the mad scientist in us who stretches Reason taut over struts
and stricken looks and doubts that one can hold a wing in mind
                                  long enough.

1986

Dream of Eileen

Eileen's Death had his arms around my neck.
We were dancing a slow dance.
He didn't mention Eileen, and neither did I.
The music stopped. He thanked me
and I sat down next to Eileen's mother, patting her knee
as she searched in her purse for a Kleenex.

Now Eileen is dancing.
She is wearing the white dress her mother picked out.
Spots of pink flush her cheeks. She is smiling at
something he has said as they pass in a swirl of white.
He's only a man. I want to tell her,
I've seen him at all these dances.

1986

The Art of Sleeping Alone

Go limp, he learned, and early morning he would find himself
lifting of someone's free will, with the mild unconcern of a foetus
in a bottle being tipped: in this position—curled with his knees
drawn up—he traveled, drifting a few feet off the ground, 4 a.m.

By then the sky was light, it being June, the neighbor's field
grown a shaggy green as he floated down the long rutted drive,
the black Lab barking and running in circles, it didn't recognize
this sleeping man who, naked and slowly turning in the air,
somehow bumped along the side of the barn and ended up
tucked under the eaves: bobbing there, chin to chest, until he woke.

This sleeping alone was no good.

Once he truly flew, or rather the universe—windless and starless—
flew past, faster than any species of fear, until he tumbled into
a room and watched his sister-in-law, whom he hadn't seen in
                                        years,
bend over a sink and rinse her hair.

Once or twice it escaped—the technique of surrender—and pursuit
climaxed in a tangle of sheets the sleeper mistook

for the wings & buckles & straps of da Vinci's contraption,
but the moment he let himself sag, and weigh what he weighed,
he felt himself rise.

Then for months he didn't fly, or even try to:
perhaps he'd mastered the art? His dreams changed.
One night he turned in his sleep, and dreaming a woman there
                                        beside him
—her sloping ribs, the jut of her hip—he stretched out an arm
and laid his hand on a distant hill.

1986

Alphabet Pyjamas

KNOT IN A PIECE OF STRING

I'm familiar with miracles, the breaking of spells:
the heart-broken mind, like a no-good
toy flung to the linoleum
suddenly works! Starts to march back and forth, a fine
little soldier, perfectly capable of dousing small fires
and cleaning its rifle.

TOY SNAKE WANTS TO SAY SOMETHING

At home I had a snake, white chalk links
under chipped green paint
and I teased it Oh! into a coil so tight
Snake couldn't speak, his blunt head
gagging on the plug of red clay they gave him for a tongue,
poor thing.

THE CONSCIOUS MIND

Water can be fooled, it smells the bitter bark of the willow
as you whittle a forked switch, and grows curious
when you wander aimlessly about,
holding the switch out in front of you:
luring the underground water—blind as a mole—
towards a freshly-dug well where you keep it: an oily shimmer,
a distant splash.

1986

DAPHNE MARLATT
b. 1942

Rings, iii.

And the bath is a river, in the quiet, i bring only candle
light, in the corner by the faucet, shadows leaping, steam.
& the window. Outside a fresh wind is frothing the apple tree,
its own river streaming, round the house,
                                    like a dream,
There is no story only the telling with no end in view or,
born headfirst, you start at the beginning & work backwards.

It was a dream, a report in the newspaper Norman was reading
(it was reported of him telling) he was born in the small
house / shack at the back of 443 Windsor (the street where
we lived—it must have been in the 100's) a big old tree,
dust, & the dilapidation of the main house where they later
lived, all this against a very blue sky that belonged to the
girl the paper said had come out to the coast for health reasons
& stayed, fell in love with the mountains & sea & made frequent
trips by ferry to the island
                        (& Al was on the phone i was
saying but feel the ribs of the baby you can feel them in me
(ribs? his or mine? contractions of muscle, something muscly
& unborn
            that she had in some way redeemed him, he painted
for her or whatever he did that was to make the paper report
his beginning.

                    & when i woke up i remembered that Norman had
        drowned in a river in the interior in his teens. But not before
i'd thought the past is still alive & grows itself so easily
i must set it down, pre-dawn of a sunny day, Wet, birds in the
half dark singing, trees only just beginning to unfold their
leaves . . .
            the sea, ferry she was on, small, crossing it, the
sea he looked down on, was the ease of his telling it, where
he is.
        In the bath a sea my belly floats in, i float
relieved of his weight—he floats within. & the genetic
stream winds backward in him, unknown, son of a father once
fathered.

Tell him, in the bath in the quiet (wind & the bell
clanging outside) only this restless streaming night, fresh
wind off the sea, is where he is. Water, candle changing in
the draft, turns slowly cool. Ripples when i lift my fingers
edge around this streaming, in the river-sea outside that winds
around our time, this city, his father's father . . .

                                                'delivered'
is a coming into THIS stream. You start at the beginning
& it keeps on beginning.

1971

Femina

        you who
                fail,
                        subtly seeking, with your face
angled downward to the floor, to cups, to broom
slivers in the cracks, to sea below, to the
hands & feet of people walking in proximity to you.
Who wait, up in your room that sideways to the
street holds certain figures in a gloom.

When the whiteness of light casts its sheen over
your face, you sit reading. & your eyes seem closed
in their downward looking, in the electric
enumeration of eyes of strangers reading you.
& bed posts, glutted with the heads of fishing
corks, which you, as yet, can still hold onto.

All
      evening
                air slowly darkened round the windows
you were caught in, rings, on a glass jar. Coherent
images of light fisted into themselves after the
bulb had gone, just, out . . . (*then* the rock cod
drift up thru blankets of the sea to reach you . . .

They flung the door open onto the city. You saw
her framed: her long. bream. skirt. ankle-tied,
heels poised on your fire-escape. The precision of

those heels. Paused, in third position, knees bent,
one fishy sleeve out, to the door . . .

                              O the fabulous
laugh of the sea trapt in a jar (o the tearing of
water.

          You are there
                         bristles of the broom are there

The bones of your face are pinned with autographs.

1972

Avebury awi-spek, *winged from buried (egg*

nose stuffed eyes holes in the chalk ridge of sinal bones rushed
down back roads' upland grass wind weaving snakelike through.
old English words: the land, the land. *man's life like the life of cereals.*
woman's too.

bring to this place the line of a life (palm says it), motive in
currents of changing weather, angst, cold for this time of year

—& small, toy pistol in one hand, cupped, & sheltered by the
pelvic thrust of rock, jumps, gotcha mom!

                                        as if to fix it
(*sine*), that jubilant ego in the face of stone, of wind flocking grey
wethers *still gathered like* (but not the same, not these) sarsens
now in place, immutable from long time back. & front, weathered
yes, in folds acquiring character we read in, clothed & prickling
now along the hairless spine, a line meeting a circle, two in one
so huge (small hill) barely visible at grass view, red windbreaker
fleck a sea of green & climb some moat in his imagination scaled
he calls me to: come & get me

                              the, all-powerful tickle,
gulp, wriggle gulping in the whole world hugged in ecstatic limit,
breath's. nothing still, no duration now (a line) creeps through
fields of (waves of) renewed green, cloud, light.

what was it they got? craniums & long bones in long barrows, construction tools from 4000 years back, *antler picks, rakes, & some ox shoulderblade shovels.* what perspective from that elevation? *matrix of chalk block walls arranged in the pattern of a spider's web* around & over a mound of turves, *grass still pliable though brown in colour . . . beetles . . . flying ants with their wings* showed them buried late July of 2660 B.C. why?

the line hypothesized druid lore (in Christian times), today a collective need to endure winter to spring, when *from his knoll . . . / the Serpent will come from his hole/ on the Brown Day of Bride,* singing, wave on wave emerging: & at centre, earth, only earth.

narrative is a strategy for survival. so it goes—transformative sinuous sentence emerging even circular, cyclic Avebury, April-May leaps *winged* from *buried.* sheds lives, laps, folds, these identities, sine: fold of a garment/ chord of an arc (active misreading). writing in monumental stones, open, not even capstone or sill, to sky (-change). *she lives* stands for nothing but this longstanding matter in the grass, settled hunks of mother crust, early Tertiary, bearing the rootholes of palms. they bring us up, in amongst stone-folds, to date: the enfolded present waits for us to have done with hiding-&-seeking terrors, territories, our obsession with the end of things.

how hug a stone (mother) except nose in to lithic fold, the old slow pulse beyond word become, under flesh, mutter of stone, *stane, stei*-ing power.

1983

prairie

in this land the rivers carve furrows and canyons as sudden to the eye as if earth opened up its miles and miles of rolling range, highway running to its evercoming horizon, days of it, light picking flowers. your blackeyed susans are here, my coral weed in brilliant patches, and always that grass frayed feathery by the season, late, and wild canada geese in the last field. i imagine your blue eye gathering these as we go, only you are not here and the parched flat opens up: badlands and hoodoos and that river with dangerous currents you cannot swim, TREACHEROUS BANK, sandstone caving in: and there she goes, Persephone caught in a whirlwind the underside churns up, the otherwise of where we are, cruising earth's surface, gazing on it, grazing, like those 70 million year old dinosaurs, the whole herd browsing the shore of Bearpaw Sea which ran all the way in up here, like Florida, she said, came in from the desert region they were hungry for grass (or flowers) when something like a flashflood caught them, their bones, all these years later, laid out in a whirlpool formation i cannot see (that as the metaphor) up there on the farthest hoodoo, those bright colours she keeps stressing, the guy in the red shirt, metal flashing, is not Hades but only the latest technician in a long line of measurers. and earth? i have seen her open up to let love in, let loose a flood, and fold again, so that even my fingers could not find their way through all that bush, all that common day rolling unbroken.

1984

kore

no one wears yellow like you excessive and radiant storehouse of sun, skin smooth as fruit but thin, leaking light. (i am climbing toward you out of the hidden.) no one shines like you, so that even your lashes flicker light, amber over blue (*amba*, amorous Demeter, you with the fire in your hand, i am coming to you). no one my tongue burrows in, whose wild flesh opens wet, tongue seeks its nest, amative and nurturing (here i am you) lips work towards undoing (*dhei*, female, sucking and suckling, fecund) spurt/ spirit opening in the dark of earth, *yu!* cry jubilant excess, your fruiting body bloom we issue into the light of, sweet, successive flesh . . .

1984

PAULETTE JILES
b. 1943

Waterloo Express

The Waterloo Express is big and important with its
glass eye, the eye of a fanatic. Sometimes they are

so important they pass you by, headed for a great
destination and bending the rails into a pure musical phrase.

Snatched loose from my baggage and address, goodbyes falling
away in flakes of dead skin, you'd say I was a high

pariah, sleepless and nowhere to go. Who do you think
I am? I bet you think I'm running away from home or

a man who never done me wrong. I bet you think
I'm twenty, with the fragile soul of a wild fawn.

Well, I used to think so too, but the job didn't pay much
and anyhow I never liked the taste of wages.

I like it here in the middle element where this
express is ripping up the dawn like an old ticket

whose engine is blowing the towns away
and even I am barely holding on.

There they go—a toe, a finger, my coat—honey,
you'd hardly recognize me, pared down to one white eye.

It has the cynical glint of a dynamite salesman.

1984

Dallas

The Washita Mountains crack a long, green eye
As we elbow through in a square and sober semi:
They are only half-awake in their rumpled bedclothes,
Gouges, humps and bluffs.
This is the hour in the earth's cycle
When metabolisms have run down:
The predator is fed up with chasing, the long-legged runner's
Long legs are folded like jackstraws in a windfall.
The rasping gawks of an early sleeper.

The driver is a corncob.
My companion is asleep.

I am a fellow-traveller to ten forward gears
And a Georgia overdrive.
Outside the sweetgrass grows as high as rain
And the morning constellations spin on a stem
Of heat that rises from the plains,

Plains that were flat before
The sea was even salt.
We are gearing down the grades that begin
The long launch to Dallas.
Texas is not my fault.
Sunshine pours from both sides of the horizon at once,
The flyspecked cabwindows are cathedrals of open light.
I am dirty, I am comfortable, I have my boots on.
Sliding down onto the blank and shadeless plains
That burn and burn like chili peppers,
We are deadheading to murderous Dallas.

1984

Lanterns

This is the hour of candlelighting; still
          cloud-shadows marble the sea
and the next island's mountain peak stands up at last
above vast, milky clouds. Even through the blue sheets
I can see the islanders of Tenerife
striking blue matches into kerosene lamps
with their glittering oils, the tiny thumbs of candles,
gothic lanterns, tin and stiff.
They are the lanterns for people
who have nobody with.
The tide drags off green and clear with salt in the empty places.
My lantern's yellow atmosphere
floats me off into space, a saint or an astronaut,
bent on getting to unknown terrain
by moonrise.

Dearest companion,
around your immobile figure the traffic of dreams sticks and jams
and even the candlelight sinks to a standstill.

The money has not come in for weeks, boats leave repeatedly
without me, full of baggage and well-heeled Swedes.
Across the sea I can imagine a continent
of my old habits, disasters, desertions—
geometric and huge, the wrong side of a moon.
None of it can touch me now, not
as long as I have my magic lantern;
a light that peels off other lights,
splitting day from night and clarifying
the limits of my territory.
It shines through my skin until I am
a tracery of ribs, a map of veins,
the red coagulation of a heart.

1984

Paper Matches

    My aunts washed dishes while the uncles
squirted each other on the lawn with
    garden hoses. Why are we in here,
I said, and they are out there?
    That's the way it is,
    said Aunt Hetty, the shrivelled-up one.

    I have the rages that small animals have,
being small, being animal.
    Written on me was a message,
'At Your Service', like a book of
paper matches. One by one we were
taken out and struck.
    We come bearing supper,
our heads on fire.

1984

Flying Lesson

These are the wings of the airplane. They have leading edges
and cut the air like a pie-knife through a fine meringue.

These are the struts. They hold the wings to the fuselage, they
correspond to the arms of angels that you see in ancient paintings
held out in surprise or warning against wings with feathers and
no leading edges.

These are the cowlings that cover the engines and
          then the propellers,
sun-dogs, solar discs which will drag behind them
          the boxy fuselage
full of passengers, babies, canned vegetables the nurse says
we must eat, sheets of plexiglass, sleeping bags, a roll of
plastic pipe and the rest of us.

These are the skis on which we take off, smashing across the
raftered ice, their shock absorbers fed up with all this, both
propellers tuned coarse and driving at the clear air like diamond
drills, reaching for altitude, for distance and a tailwind out
of the north.

Kiss off, kiss off, O earth, O village of earth-folk down below,
waving your puffy-mitt goodbyes, we are the people of the air.
Here the milk of winter clouds is churned into our special butter.
Some day when the roads come in and cars like
          armadillos lurch up
their frozen byways,

remember we once flew like legends in these frail kites. Remember
us, a boreal airborne royalty. Remember some of us died.

And these are the dials of the flight deck.
This is the vertical speed indicator, this is the radar, at night
hissing in green sweeps, the oil pressure and the bank-and-turn.
This is the altimeter which tells us of the earth, now drawing

up in a snowy flow, where we owe a life, despite the aviation
of souls. We return in our damp fur and parkas toward an
artificial horizon, to everything that is
unjust, unpaid-for and unwarranted,
claimed by our bodies like baggage,
we, the earth-people,
descend again.

1984

The Mystic

God is only a symbol for life, for
fate or potatoes.
For missing persons smiling out of photographs.
He is more desperate and more commonplace
than once thought. Why is it
we have to fight our way out of
darkness and miscalculation like
a lost patrol in a banana jungle, only
    to discover this,
      the Potato God?

Ah, sweet animism, the silent crystals
at the core of things,
like baseballs and shells, new potatoes,
waiting for moisture, to spring
on you, rains
    of carbon and cut glass.

1984

Living Alone

The earth folds up her grasses.
Starshine strikes like the appearance of aliens.
The aurora is a piano, playing blues
in green neon. The junked taxi sinks
into the asters.

In the centre of all this noisy brilliance
is a cabin silence and absence.

Sometimes you spoon-feed the soul,
silence in small sips,
a sort of dole, you
put it on relief.

Foxtail grass turns gravely on its spears.
Shut up, wait for the angel or the airplane
disguised as an angel to descend
with silent twin propellers out of the
madonna-blue evening, wait for

your cue, your
moment to appear in the
zodiacal footlights of
this special and dreadful
one-man show.

1984

BRONWEN WALLACE
b. 1945

Melons at the Speed of Light

For Carolyn Smart

*'Child,' said the lion, 'I am telling you your story, not hers. No-one is
told any story but their own'*
—C.S. LEWIS, *A Horse and his Boy.*

I keep having this dream
where the women I love swell up like melons,
    night after night.
It's not surprising, really.
They've reached that age
where a woman must decide once and for all,
and this summer most of them are pregnant.
Already their eyes have changed.
Like those pools you discover once in a while,
so deep with themselves
you can't imagine anything else swimming in them.
The eyes of pregnant women. The women I love
fallen into themselves, somehow, far beyond calling,
as if whatever swims in their bellies
were pulling them deeper and deeper.

I think that women's lives
are like our bodies.
Always at the mercy, you might say.
A woman turns 32 and her body lets her know
it's time to decide.
Or maybe she just loses her job and can't find another
so she figures she might as well have the babies now as later.

The days become all mouth then
and everything smells of milk.
Her body goes a little vague at the edges
like it felt that time at summer camp
when she was learning how to hang in the water
      without moving.
'Drown-proofing', they called it.
Said it could hold you up for hours.
These are the days that slow
to the pace of glass,
the world outside a silent, lazy smudge
on the horizon somewhere.
'After my son was born,' a friend told me,
'in those first few months, whenever he was asleep,
I'd spend hours putting on makeup,
just so I could touch my own face again,
just so I knew I was there.'

In the dreams they are green and determined,
growing larger by the minute, and there's something
I need to warn them about before it's too late,
but they go on ripening without me.
So far, I always find myself awake
before anything else happens,
hands in the dry night, exploring the bed
for a mess of pulp and seeds.

Meanwhile, my son turns ten this summer.
Every morning, he plays baseball in the park next door,
leaving me quiet for coffee and the paper.
But it never works. It's his voice, rising
through the noise of the game, that shapes me still,
the way, years earlier, his turning knotted my belly,
the kick under my ribs, aimed at the heart.
When I take my coffee to the bleachers, he ignores me.
He's the smallest boy on his team, but he's got a good arm.
The coach gives him third base, usually, or shortstop.
Right field is a demotion. I can tell he feels it
by his walk, though his face shows nothing.
It's like the sadness in his wrists when he's up to bat,
knowing he'll manage a good base hit, probably, but never
      a home run.
He's the kind of player every coach needs on the team

and, watching him stretch for a fly ball, I can see
how I'm the one who needs to grow up.
I carried him like the future, unmarked, malleable,
but what I gave birth to isn't like that at all,
isn't a life I can decide for any more.
This is what my son knows already;
he just wants to get on with it.

What I get on with is this dream
where women swell up like melons,
ready to ripen or burst.
I want to believe I am dreaming for my friends,
for all the things I'd tell them if I could.
How they are bound by this birth forever
to the lives of other women, to a love
that roots itself as deeply
as our need for the earth.
I want to tell them this
is an old, old story,
but of course they can't listen.
They are ripening into their own versions of it
as if it had never happened to anyone else before.
These women I love so much.
Their recklessness. Like that fly ball
at the speed of light
stinging into my son's glove.

1985

Common Magic

Your best friend falls in love
and her brain turns to water.
You can watch her lips move,
making the customary sounds,
but you can see they're merely
words, flimsy as bubbles rising
from some golden sea where she
swims sleek and exotic as a mermaid.

It's always like that.
You stop for lunch in a crowded

restaurant and the waitress floats
toward you. You can tell she doesn't care
whether you have the baked or french-fried
and you wonder if your voice comes
in bubbles too.

It's not just women either. Or love
for that matter. The old man
across from you on the bus holds
a young child on his knee; he is singing
to her and his voice is a small boy
turning somersaults in the green
country of his blood.
It's only when the driver calls his stop
that he emerges into this puzzle
of brick and tiny hedges. Only then
you notice his shaking hands, his need
of the child to guide him home.

All over the city
you move in your own seasons
through the seasons of others: old women, faces
clawed by weather you can't feel
clack dry tongues at passersby
while adolescents seethe
in their glassy atmospheres of anger.

In parks, the children
are alien life-forms, rooted
in the galaxies they've grown through
to get here. Their games weave
the interface and their laughter
tickles that part of your brain where smells
are hidden and the nuzzling textures of things.

It's a wonder that anything gets done
at all: a mechanic flails
at the muffler of your car
through whatever storm he's trapped inside
and the mailman stares at numbers
from the haze of a distant summer.

Yet somehow letters arrive and buses
remember their routes. Banks balance.
Mangoes ripen on the supermarket shelves.
Everyone manages. You gulp the thin air
of this planet as if it were the only
one you knew. Even the earth you're
standing on seems solid enough.
It's always the chance word, unthinking
gesture that unlocks the face before you.
Reveals the intricate countries
deep within the eyes. The hidden
lives, like sudden miracles,
that breathe there.

1985

Joseph MacLeod Daffodils

For Isabel Huggan

'I'm planting perennials this year,' you tell me,
'because I'm scared and it's the only way I know
to tell myself I'm going to be here,
years from now, watching them come up.'
Maybe it's a phase we're going through,
since I'm at it too; lily of the valley,
under the back hedge, thinking *when Jeremy*
is old enough to drive, I'll have to divide these,
put some under the cedars there: by the time
he leaves home, they'll be thick as grass.
and at the same time saying
'God, we're parodies of ourselves,
sixties children, still counting on flowers,
for chrissake, to get us through.'
Knowing you'll see it that way too,
your snort of laughter
the index of my love and the wisdom
of George Eliot's observation that
'a difference of taste in jokes
is a great strain on the affections'.
(Another thing we share, our delight
in quotations like that, exactly what you'd expect
from girls who grew up wearing glasses

into women who read everything;
your bathroom so much like mine,
a huge bin of books by the toilet
and on the shelves, all the bottles
turned label side out.
'The contents of somebody's bathroom,'
Diane Arbus said, 'is like reading their biography.')
This doesn't help much, does it?
You're laughing, but your hands stay
clenched in your lap, still forcing
the tight, dumb bulbs into the ground
as if you could force your life
to a pattern as serene as theirs,
a clam that flourishes in darkness
to the pull of the sun.
Still, I keep on talking.
It's the only wisdom that I've got.
How about this one: you know those
big, yellow daffodils—they're called
Joseph MacLeods—well, the way they got their name
was that the man who developed them
always kept a radio on in the greenhouse
and the day the first one bloomed, in 1942,
was the day he got the news
of the Allied victory, against Rommel,
at El Alamein, and the announcer who read the news
was Joseph MacLeod. Which shows a sense of history
I can appreciate; no *El Alamein Glorias* or
Allied Victory Blooms for this guy, you can be sure.
It's like the story my mother always tells
about joining the crowds on V-E day, swollen with me,
but dancing all night, thinking *now*
she can be born any time.

What I love
is how these stories try to explain
the fit of things, though I can see
your mood's for something more sinister.
Like the reason Diane Arbus gave
for photographing freaks, maybe?
'Aristocrats', she called them,
'They've already passed their test in life.'

Being born with their trauma, that is,
while the rest of us must sit around, dreading it.
Meaning you and me. *Normal*. Look at us,
practically wizened with worry, hunched
over coffee cups, whispering of cancer and divorce,
something happening to one of the kids, our lives
spread between us like those articles you read
about Mid-Life Crisis or Identity Anxiety,
Conflict of Role Expectations in Modern Marriages,
the kind that tell you you can fix all that
with less red meat and more exercise,
the ones that talk as if the future's
something you decide about,
though what it all comes down to, every time,
is making do. You can call it a choice
if you want, but that doesn't change
what we learn to rely on,
the smaller strategems. Whatever works.
The socks in their neat balls, tucked on the right
side of the drawer, the iris coming up each summer
in the south bed. 'Be sincere and don't fuss'.
'Noble deeds and hot baths
are the best cures for depression'.

It's what I love in you, Isabel.
How you can stand here saying
'Brave and kind. I want to get through this
being brave and kind', squaring your shoulders
like a heroine in those movies our mothers watched
where people knew their problems
didn't amount to a hill of beans
in this crazy world and let it go at that,
fitting themselves to the shape
a life makes for itself without meaning to.
I love your grin from the end of my sidewalk
as you head for home, posed like a photograph.
'Perfectly Ordinary Woman on Suburban Street'.
'A secret about a secret', Arbus called this kind,
'the more it tells you,
the less you know.'

1988

LIBBY SCHEIER
b. 1946

There Is No Such Thing as Silence,

in the longest and deepest silences I hear my organs heaving and
hauling in their daily labors, moving blood and tissues, inhaling /
exhaling, perceiving, touching, sensing—what noise, what noise the
body makes when the mind is listening, and in the deepest silences
the mind foments raucous storms, sometimes it zings out the same
string of lightning ten times, then a thick black cloud descends, hum-
ming, it lifts and the sun goes pop a few times like a specially bred
dog, a dog bred to be small and whiny and weak and delicate, the
sun goes pop pop, weak like a chihuahua.

so it is a myth about silences, there are no silences, whenever you
desire with all your heart a great silence and start to sink into it, you
sink into the splash and plash of the body and the bang and pop of
the mind.

why are there no silences? we desire nothing so much as a perfect
long black silence. but life is filled with noise. I suspect that death too
is noisy. what is this yearning for silence? perhaps it is the rock in
me, the ancient lava, the sea floor, the hardness and roundness of my
skull like a boulder, and my bones like petrified wood that lies quiet
in dark forests. perhaps it is the sea salt in my blood, the salty blood
in motion like the sea.

bones bring us back to the silence of minerals, the hardness of
stone. bones are only invaded by marrow, a noisy substance, full of
direction and self-interest and the need to survive.

follow the human fetus as it develops. it justifies darwin and repro-
duces the evolution of the species. tail, gills, whatever you want. and
at early stages the sex organs are the same in female and male. later
the little bump becomes clitoris or penis, the shapeless folds become
labia or scrotum. like our ancestral ameba, we pass through andro-
gyny, or, to be clearer, the absence of gender.

as the stages of the fetus prove our lack of species originality, prove
our link with all animal life, so do the bones, the skeleton that survives
after body death, prove our oneness with the elements of silence, with
the minerals that rested here before the commotion of cell life began.

I want to tap into my bones tonight, I want to drain the marrow,
I want to tap into the silence.

1986

Penises, 1

Freud never had one.

We're irritated with penises.
The psychiatrists
have shoved them down our throats for too long.
Penis envy and other silliness.
So there's backlash.

Penises are kind of a pain because
they're so vulnerable hanging out there like that
and men are so concerned about the way they hang
out there like that.
Penises are not consistent.
They make foolish demands
or lapse into abject defeatism.
They know no happy medium.
Penises are Jewish:
When they fail they transfer the guilt,
when they succeed they take all the glory.

Penises are funny.
Sylvia said they look like chicken gizzards.
I said sausage and eggs
old monkey skin
and hairs of an elephant's head.
Let's face it.
Penises are not goodlooking.
They can be fun, but they're never pretty.

Penises hang on grown men.
Children do not have penises.
Or so I thought.

But I had a baby boy.
He has a penis.
It's small and pretty like a little finger.
He does not yet have a piece of his brain
in the head of his penis.
Some days he wants to be a girl.
Some days he wants to be a boy.
It's no big deal for him.

He is intensely interested in trucks, trains, airplanes, boats,
crayons, paint, playdough, books, bikes, wagons, puppets, hats,
necklaces, blocks, dolls, doll carriages, rabbits, and nail polish—
which he insists on wearing ever since he saw it
on the fingernails of a friend of mine.
He doesn't confuse his interest in trucks with his penis.
He doesn't confuse his fondness for nail polish with his penis.
He pees with his penis.
He plays with it.
He likes playing with it.
He likes aiming his piss
and he likes his little erections.
But he's big on his feet and toes too.
And he greatly admires his belly button.
Let's face it.
He's got his penis in perspective.
It's part of the body.

Penis envy is a theory
that came from Freud's problem
which was a compulsive obsession
with penises
which was not surprising since he never had one.

As part of the male body,
the penis is quite a nice part.
Functional, humorous, unpredictable.
As container for the entire male body
including the brain
the penis in this case is a bore.

*with apologies to bpNichol and
his wonderful poem, 'The Vagina'*

1986

Five Meditations on Jungles

I

Singular vines coil skyward
large voluptuous leaves catch
more sunlight than I've ever seen

in one place, the rough cantilevered bark
is almost effective armour
for the sweet and chunky juice
of its interior
dark dark at the base the tree
stretches intently toward the perfect
brightness of the sky

2

How do I find myself suddenly
enveloped in the imagery
of the jungle? I realize I
have had next to nothing to do with
the imagery of the jungle, I could
make easy analysis and see myself
plunged into a yearning for the
primitive, for physical and wordless love.

3

The crazy geometry of the zebra.
Does this kind of exactness belong
on an animal that runs with grace
and eats green leaves?

4

Now I have to ask myself why stripes
in the jungle strike me as incongruous.
So I ask and the answer has something
to do with romantic idealism and
yearnings for circles and absence
of boundaries. Stripes are manmade things
affixed to military paraphernalia like
flags and men's shoulders.
Someone points out that the stripes on
zebras and snakes and tigers are
mostly circles, not out of sync with the jungle
or my image of the jungle.

5

Jungles have intense light
and intense darkness where beauty

can exist in total secrecy
unspoiled by versifiers and image-makers.
This is how it was intended to be.
For what's dark to remain dark.
For what's light to dazzle.

1986

Women

Women are going blind from too much data
and the lean beginnings of truth
starting as the skin of a dead cactus
against a surface of flesh made raw
ending somewhere far into the dark canals
of children's dreams, ending somewhere
near the end of the tunnel where we give up
looking for the stark white light of the exit
and start digging into the walls
with our hands, eating
through the rock of the mountain
travelling slowly toward the blue sky
travelling slowly toward the beautiful
bodies of our naked children
our women and our men
slithering through the long measure of stone,
saintly worms, wet and subversive,
travelling slowly until our bodies open suddenly
like clamshells or dinosaur eggs
and in the mountain air against the sky
we see each other with open eyes
what we really look like.
What we are.

1986

SHARON THESEN
b. 1946

A, An, The

You go to the Planetarium
and do some shopping
& then you have a coffee.

You cannot bear to read any more prose
and after the second cup of coffee
you get a pain in the lower left side.

You have taken your car in for a tune-up
and may have to wait another day
before getting it back.

You have nothing to say
and your part is crooked
and your books are overdue at the library.

You take a dress to the cleaners
& then you catch the bus
and look out the window with your purse.

●
The oak tree
deciphers November.
It breathes & leaves,
branches fall.
The dry sound
of their scattering
descent is of crumpled
paper surrounding the heart
of someone composing
a Dear John letter.
Piling up along the boundary
where earth meets
underground, lanterns
lighting a somewhat cheerful
way, until the

however
of the second sentence.

1987

Eclipse Calypso

The weekend weather report
shivers in the azure.
Humans wired for sound
don't dawdle, pale demographs
wearing flags of defeated art,
paying for metric pork chops
& the 3rd world—who am I
to say they don't even know how to sing
let alone flip a pancake
in the log hut where Ma, Pa
and a zillion kids
swarm? All warm?—

While the strictures of the lyric
huddle in the aether
fumbling with matches, trying
to do something with language

As if some thing were a dead thing
or your own heart a satire
upon the soon-to-be-eclipsed
innocent moon—the old girl

is such a gorgeous hostess tonight
in platinum brocade by Bill Blass,
her slightly crooked, semiological grin
drives earth crazy!

With a predictable shady desire,
my dear,
a predictable shady desire.

1987

The Occasions

Men have talked about the world
without paying attention to the world
or to their own minds, as if
they were asleep or absent-minded.
— HERACLITUS

Are dim. Are a missing
of the mark. Are pretty
Chinese lanterns, fireworks
I woke to thinking
someone was stealing the piano.
Are the piano itself;
Moments musicaux
fall out of the window, scatter
like mercury all over everything.

In the Public Garden someone bends
over the roses. But for the polar bears,
orangutans, sea otters,
purple-ass baboons, the giraffe,
crocodiles, peacocks, the killer whale,
the zoo is deserted. Under the water
creatures blink and eat.

These pale pink roses
are the tenderest things.
The palest alabaster pink.
Sitting with them you understand
the perfection of all things.

Moments later amnesia, *rubato*
of a phrase of light.

2

The phone rings, hauling you up
out of a dream. You are lightheaded,
unreal, addicted to whatever
keeps you going. Books, coffee,
poetry, someone's voice.

Across town the carpenters
lay down their tools &

drive away in dusty Thunderbirds
to a meeting in the stadium.
Someone explains his situation
at the Food Bank. Someone else
closes the curtains & opens the Scotch.
The intermittent sun
exhales a yellow breath.
Clockwise, tiny black aphids
race around the convolutions
of a rose someone aims at
with a spray gun.

The convolutions of the rose
suggest an ecstasy
untroubled by too much meaning.

Or too little.

Outside the Hudson's Bay
the Hare Krishnas are hopping
and chanting; unburdened,
ecstatic, their blue invisible deities
laugh in the air.

3

Greek Day. The Pericles Society
Souvlaki Stand runs out early.
Solemn bouzouki bands
repeat themselves in faster measures
for the young men who dance,
naked insteps flashing among the swords,
handsome conceited heads flicking
to the left and the right.
Old mothers in black click & talk
the meat smoke rises
as if from ancient battlegrounds.
Heraclitus, dog-bitten old ghost
admonishes the crowd
to wake up & share a world
as a small plane
trailing a river of plastic words
progresses round the sky.

4

Speaking English
we go over & over
the things that happen,
but I would rather have you
in my arms than in this conversation.

Desire and ineptitude
commit themselves to memory—
it's hard not to regret
anything. For example
coldness, a pretended indifference.
The heart transformed
to a battery.

Pairs of women
lean over restaurant tables
talking. They know everything.
Their perfume recalls to them
a certain gesture in the back seat
of a taxi in Toronto that said
I agree to this.

They fiddle with their earrings,
sufficient unto themselves
in pale summer dresses
like women who wait
for a war to end.

Or the shrimp boats
to come in. So why don't you
hurry home. The windows
are open: one to the east
& one to the west. Sirens
in the cross-breeze,
novels on the bed.

1987

MARLENE NOURBESE PHILIP
b. 1947

Testimony Stoops to Mother Tongue

'Tis a figure, a symbol, say;
a thing's sign: now for the thing signified
— ROBERT BROWNING, *The Ring and the Book*

I

Stone mourns
                    haunted
into shape and form
by its loss
          upon
                loss
honed keen
as the feel of some days
at the very centre of every word,
the as-if of yesterday it happened;
mind and body concentrate
                                    history—
the confusion of centuries that passes
as the word
            kinks hair
            flattens noses
            thickens lips
            designs prognathous jaws
            shrinks the brain
to unleash the promise
                            in ugly
the absent in image.

II

those who would
                    inhabit
the beyond of pale
where the sacrilege of zero
                            disputes
the mathematic of heart,
erect shrines of stone to the common
                                    in us
          —anathema—

touch tongue to tongue
                              release
the strange sandwiched between
tongue and cheek and lip

III

the somewhere of another mother's tongue

                                        tongues

                                                licks

into nothing
the prison of these walled tongues
—speaks
              this/
              fuck-mother motherfuckin-
              this/
              holy-white-father-in-heaven-
              this/
              ai! ai!
                        tongue
that wraps
      squeezes
the mind round
                        and around

IV

this tongue that roots
                              deep
in
    yank
    pull
    tear
    root
out
that I would
                  chop
                        in
pieces
        a snake
each to grow
                  a head
(Gorgon-

to turn my tongue to stone)
        a tail
and haunt the absence
        that mourns
/haunted into shape and form . . . . .

v

Oh, but shall I?
        I shall
tame them—
        these snakes
feed them
        milk
from black breasts
        (stroke and caress into
lactate)
        to hush
the slithered silk of tongues
        split
—shiver and silver into forty pieces—
words ride again
        across
mared nights

let me—
        I shall
lie
  with them
  bed them with silence
these snakes
        wisdomed
with the evil
        of words
to breed the again and
again
    in breed
—a new breed
—a race
—a warrior race
        of words
—a nest-egg
        that waits

to hatch the ever
                    in wait

VI

shall I
       strike
under tongue and foot
them
       —these words
hold in aloft
                up
in either hand
                harmless
the word
           that claims
and maims
               and claims
again
or
       in my mother's mouth
       shall I
                use
the father's tongue
cohabit in strange
mother
           incestuous words
           to revenge the self
                           broken
upon
      the word

1988

ROSEMARY SULLIVAN
b. 1947

The Fugitive Heart

Today he brought his heart to us in a black bag.
It looked like an ocharina huddled beside a silver flute,
a fat orange bulb with holes to blow on.

He slipped it out when we weren't looking
and it sat in the corner watching us.

It was wary, his orphan heart, careful of exits,
dreaming of women and kisses.
It wrapped itself around the table leg
and talked of life under bridges
where stray children fucked dogs for food.
A hungry heart with knives in its fingers,
scouring the streets for women to sell.

When you kill and you hear the soft hiss
of life leak from the body,
the heart looks itself in the face.
It sees only a fat sponge
that sucks the air with blood.
"So that's life," he said.

I watched his eyes retreat to the back of his face;
the heart on the table now,
a taut grey sack.
He picked it up delicately
like a blister
and put it back inside his coat.

1986

Sisters

Each summer when the others left for camp
we carted the mattress to the backyard
to build our tent — an eerie laundry
hanging in the moonlight.

I was thirteen months behind you,
watching from a distance the body
you ran to meet so suddenly
those nights we lay in cooling dark

listening to the crickets drumming
the pulse of summer, the moon
an old woman leaning
through cracks in our blanket walls.

Your body was the mystery I waited for
from my childish space, the bones
shifting slowly like some creature
surfacing inside you.

Your breast spots stretching you
out of my world
the night he called you
took off his clothes carefully

a ritual danced in moonlight,
daring you to come out;
you only laughed
and told me never to tell.

I did, of course, caught off balance
in that zone families clear
for a middle child —
perhaps it was then I cut my face

from all the family photos —
when I look at them now
there is always a small hole
sitting in the corner

I started spelling my name backwards,
retreating from the space a name makes.
Kind with my betrayal,
you understood the child roaming sadly in a body.

The tent gone, another summer;
the creature stretched me too
as I watched night after night
the mirror, alone in my room.

You are still the guide in my dreams
teaching me to leap gaps between spaces,
still the loved one waiting patiently
for the childish dreamer to catch you.

1986

Words

Aunt Mary used to warn me about words.
They never stay where you put them.
They're loose.
Any no-good can use them.
Like a woman, she tried
to keep them safe in the family.

Family was her story that added down to me
— always fenced with a lesson:
Words break loose if you let them.

She stored the family photos in a basket.
Trussed up in her rocker, warty as any gourd,
each night her hands plunged the corridors of blood.
I knew she was hooked on danger.

She could go all the way back to wind,
how it falls and picks itself up in a field.
Or fog empties a valley till all you see
is your hands where the world was.

From her I learned there were others
pacing inside me.
She said they had made me up.
I was meant to love them.

But it terrified me to think I was lived in
by strangers I had never met
or knew only by name.
They made me alien fiction.

In my bones
an old woman dies over and over.
I dare not look
in the room with the blooded axe.
Nor speak to the men who walked out.
Their tracks in my blood. Their lust
for edges.

I could spend
a lifetime digging graves
in my head.

1988

LORNA CROZIER
b. 1948

Poem About Nothing

Zero is the one we didn't understand
at school. Multiplied by anything
it remains nothing.

When I ask my friend
the mathematician who studies rhetoric
if zero is a number, he says *yes*
and I feel great relief.

If it were landscape
it would be a desert.
If it had anything to do
with anatomy, it would be
a mouth, a missing limb,
a lost organ.

Ø

Zero worms its way
                        between one and one
and changes everything.
It slips inside the alphabet.
It is the vowel on a mute tongue,
the pupil in a blind man's eye,
the image
            of the face
he holds on his fingertips.

Ø

When you look up
from the bottom of a dry well
zero is what you see,
the terrible blue of it.

It is the rope
you knot around your throat
when your heels itch for wings.

Icarus understood zero
as he caught the smell
of burning feathers
and fell into the sea.

Ø

If you roll zero down a hill
it will grow,
swallow the towns, the farms,
the people at their tables
playing tic-tac-toe.

Ø

When the Cree chiefs
signed the treaties on the plains
they wrote *X*
beside their names.

In English, X equals zero.

Ø

I ask my friend
the rhetorician who studies mathematics
What does zero mean and keep it simple.

He says *Zip.*

Ø

Zero is the pornographer's number.
He orders it through the mail
under a false name. It is the number
of the last man on death row,
the number of the girl who jumps
three stories to abort.

Zero starts and ends
at the same place. Some compare it
to driving across the Prairies all day
and feeling you've gone nowhere.

ø   ø   ø

In the beginning God made zero.

1985

We Call This Fear

We call this fear *love*, this tearing,
this fist, this sharpened tongue
love. I could kill you, I say,
many times. You do not carry
the only pain. There is more
than your world: the drunks
you find bleeding on the tiles,
the women full of holes, the dog
with torn eyes, the poet who has
chewed his tongue.

There is this room,
this woman who brings you food
wears your bruises on her cheeks.
I am tired, so tired.
There is always something wrong.
You spit words at me
like broken teeth and I, stupid
woman, string them into poems,
call them love.

1985

Fishing in Air

What he fishes for changes
as light changes on water.
Whitefish, pickerel, goldeye.
There is a space in his mind
where they die, a pier slippery with scales
where their eyes turn to slime.

His line is invisible.
He has forgotten what lure falls
endlessly through water.
It could be feathered or striped
or a silver curve that flashes
at the slightest flick of his wrist.

If he could send his eye out on a hook,
return it to its socket when he reels in the line,
he would do so. If he could use his heart for bait
then cut it from the fish within a fish.

There is something he has never caught.
Something that makes him stand here
every evening, casting, casting
and reeling in.

Every time he fishes he is different.
The water is different, the sky, the way
the tern hangs in the air or doesn't.
What he will catch is a minnow now,
slim and golden, growing to fill an emptiness
in a lake he's never seen before—
no road in or out.

1985

The Morning of the Sad Women

Morning holds its mirror
to the window, the women
wake to their own reflections,
fall into loneliness deeper

than the night they rose from.
They reach for housecoats,
brush the tangles from their hair
as if there were a chance
of meeting someone in the hall.

If it is winter, the rooms are dark.
Clocks count heartbeats
in the glow of bedside lamps.
Albums hold their secrets
in dresser drawers, press
the photographs so thin
there is little left of them.

Downstairs no one is making breakfast,
no one brings oranges on a silver tray.
Morning makes a poor companion
when there is nowhere to go with it,
when it repeats the same
conversations across the narrow table
over and over without end.

1985

From *The Sex Lives of Vegetables*

CARROTS

Carrots are fucking
the earth. A permanent
erection, they push deeper
into the damp and dark.
All summer long
they try so hard to please.
*Was it good for you,
was it good?*

Perhaps because the earth won't answer
they keep on trying.
While you stroll through the garden
thinking *carrot cake,
carrots and onions in beef stew,
carrot pudding with caramel sauce,*

they are fucking their brains out
in the hottest part of the afternoon.

CAULIFLOWER

The garden's pale brain,
it knows the secret
lives of all the vegetables,
holds their fantasies,
their green libidos
in its fleshy lobes.

PEAS

Peas never liked any of it.
They make you suffer for the sweet
burst of green in the mouth. Remember
the hours of shelling on the front steps,
the ping into the basin? Your mother
bribing you with lemonade to keep you there,
splitting them open with your thumbs.

Your tongue finds them clitoral
as it slides up the pod.
Peas are not amused.
They have spent all their lives
keeping their knees together.

1985

KRISTJANA GUNNARS
b. 1948

dwarf pear

there were trees budded
kept small
short-lived: unprofitable, they said
unworthy

they were garden dwarf trees
high-culture trees
made with hours of judicious pruning

i remember fathers gathering
the easy flourish of many years
loaded with fruit
a year from the bud

fathers who argued the incessant success

i lie in the manna grass again
remember those tall sayings
and how easily my thoughts rupture
how fast you flow out

the sloughs of loss:
was our culture then not coarse enough—
how miniature we kept our love
how we erased the wet meadows

and when the dwarf threatened to bear fruit
we thought of death, no
we thought of murder
we thought of keeping the small small love
unworthy

1985

milky way vegetation II

I

you do not know if
i do not tell you, how
i see among the grasses

lady's bedstraw, wood
cranes' bills, water avens
and wild angelica

each one appears many times
a negative of constellations

how between the print and reality
i have placed you

standing in the hawkweeds
exposed under the sky

2

between dry stretches
covered with sedges
i have been through carpets of cotton-grass
in the central highlands

between tundra bogs
ridged with gravel and stone
i have been through grasslands
heaths scattered with plants

my journeys uncharted, undated
the boundaries unmarked
the hours broken
my uncoordinated life

3

a touch of the wild thyme
and moss campion of very old
mountain-drifted freedom
appears with you

who do not know
that with you the highlands occur
showing again the old sky
approximately as it would look

to the unwarned eye

4

even while the blue and red summer nights say yes
yes

the black sands follow me
the lowlands extend barren
newly-poured lava flows down the gullet of hope

and there is continuous no on the wings of the gulls

5

after this returning, i know

the beds of moss, dwarf
shrubs, birches
rained-on

ravines of ferns and herbs
luxuriant
brilliant red stars at my fingertips

life a glowing object

1985

those subjected to radioactivity who did
not die were marked for life

the idea of storing
nuclear waste in the sea once had
a strong following
but i understand
there is not enough water in all the oceans
to cover even ten percent of our sins

today a black-capped bird
eats flies at the landing place
a young gull circles
with a rasping call

the lumpsucker season started
the day before yesterday
freshly caught fish lie
in a wagon outside the shed
and a little girl sells them, her hands folded

i hear
the banks from skagatá to langanes are open
and northern boats are out on the cold sea
too cold, they say
and the lumpsucker is late this year

again sounds the za–za of the gull
down by the broken boards
and rusty nails
today i feel particularly aware
of the possibility

that radioactivity resembles sin
it spreads unseen
through plankton, algae, fish
and i have come to buy it from a little girl
with folded hands

1985

MARILYN BOWERING
b. 1949

Gains and Losses

Winter pears, green and hard as ovaries,
were stored on the back porch.
Perhaps that is where
the women produced them, ready-made
from the womb.

Instead of babies
let us have fruit that can be kept quiet,
and eaten when required.

I am trying to tell the story:
how I found three infant mounds
and the wooden cross that grandpa made,
at Brookside: Wilbert, Clifford, Thomas
were the names.

I am opposed
to the human orchard—
    flower and be touched,
    ingest pollen and work on it
until something sweet buds and falls.

Every story comes back to its beginning:
friends move like shadows on a curtain,
and we are alone, despite the planning.

Through this ability to produce
something useful

and keep it in quantity
for a winter
when the wind
blows down the chimney
and thieves through the rooms,

children are stolen,

either in their own, or another's memory.

Let me give you an instance.
Daddy shared a bed with his brother Thomas,
Thomas died, and Daddy didn't.

Daddy grew numb with death:
having escaped it, he had the wisdom
to hate it.

Other brothers died of other things,

but he fathered me
out of this hurtful
habit of living.

1982

Well, it ain't no sin to take off your skin and dance around in your bones

I heard bones clacking last night
in the bed.
It was dreams, and not sleeping—
could it be a cold future?
There was snow on the morning ground.

I could hear skin, loose and naked
as it sloughed, layer by layer:

I liked its shape and hair and the pads
of its fingers,

but I could dance, I could dance with the bones.

Little lamb on the hillside,
you were drowning in snow,
and your ewe and shepherd danced over a stone:
warm rivers ran from those dancing feet
(black hooves and toes).

I slept badly last night,
listening to bones move like ancient wheels
over a slippery road.
They made a sound, chattering
like pebbles dropping down a mountain,

like hot streams bubbling from lava,
like a long time ago,

when there was you dancing, and me dancing.

1982

The Origin of Species: Starting Point

Let's say that the god's voice
is genuine;
that is, the brain is truly enlightened
by thoughts of it;

and that the brain is also an animal.

Let's say that they meet
at a cave entrance
neither possesses,

and further, that neither is strong:

understand that I mean there is no good
or evil.

But let's say that life is extinguished through conflict,
and, in time, is resurrected (as is so),

and that the brain betrays understanding
in a story:

it loves and tames the bull-headed monster at its centre,

and all convolutions and laminae are taken-up
with death, sacrifice and honour,

and the white and grey matter are characters,
male and female, full of grace and beauty.

At such a moment I chose you.
At such a moment there was no god or animal.

Why not now? Why not always?

1984

The Sunday Before Winter

Though not always, today cloud blanks out distance.
Memory deepens the isolation.

This love is no comfort:

night and silence double,
though true evil blunts itself on the mettle of two.

There are few links in the life of the mind
between the dreamer and his island.
We are asleep, or awaken full of longing,
and so sleep and long
until life is a tract of absence.

I will not go under its anaesthetic
(unless you permit it).
Your touch is an anodyne of trust—

this is the certainty I swim or drown in—

as the moon darkens at the perigee,

and we tell hours
in death and repayment,
invalid as a moment.

Love, life, and will
are tempered by diminishing heat,

and utter, utter annexation.

1984

MARY DI MICHELE
b. 1949

The Moon and the Salt Flats

'How I would like to believe in tenderness—'
— SYLVIA PLATH

The moon is an ivory tusk in the Utah sky
over the salt flats of ultra white.
The ground is a soft wax that receives my steps
and prints their passage. Before the Mormons
the pulse of the earth was white, the sky, marine.
The Indians spoke of it in their red dream language
of clay and old blood. Sailing for me is the angel of
tenderness.

It had been promised in books that if I were good
and prayed to the right gods I would find my heart
netted in blue pacific light, but I'm perched
unsteadily on spindly doubts and can't run.
Winged and yet a magpie whose tail is longer than her body,
I'm clumsy when I don't talk about flying.
They call me bitter tears, Mary means,

without the trace of the sea I hear in *Maria* like a shell.
Only the salt of that forgotten ocean's biography
remains a relic of powdered bone, chalk white,

Saint Sea who still can make the earth's eyes here moist
with a keen nostalgia for it. Tears, the bed of my own making,
dry and only the salt is left behind. Watch me sleep on it.
If I could get a better look at him, I'd go to the moon

switching on her deeper lights, but the moon won't have me.
All ideas are colourless and odourless and stoppered in a vial
so that they can't be dangerous to me at this moment.
My eyes are sea green, my heart is blue.
Is it love that makes the earth pirouette on his axis
and the moon perform her crab-like bow around him?
There's no looking back, *amore*,

we're the only living things growing on the salt flats.

1981

Necessary Sugar

For Emily

I watch you sleeping by the window
where the horse-chestnut lives,
its white candelabra blooms
aflame in the solemn mass
of the sun.

Giving birth I realized that men
build cathedrals in an attempt
to sculpt light,
you are the firefly
I collected between my legs.

A fiction that last summer's romance
had to write
for your father,
for myself,
not believing
love could be a lie
even if mistaken.

However the years tell this story to you
already June has ground up
the petals strewn across the walk

like a welcoming carpet for a queen
under the wheels of my shopping-cart.

My little bag of sugar, ten pounds,
I carry you in the corduroy snuggli,
my kangaroo pouch,
or the house a man might build
for his love to grow in.

1983

Hunger

(On a winter day, the body of a young girl was found at a rooming-house, in a plastic bag, stuffed into a refrigerator. In a different part of the country, the parents of another such victim offered love and forgiveness to the person responsible for their daughter's death, saying, 'We would like to know who the person or persons are so we could share, hopefully, a love that seems to be missing in these people's lives.')

For some the afternoon light
is a mess of leftover porridge,
a greying, clotted mass,
to be eaten again for dinner,
or the rye that stains the bottom
of an unwashed glass.
A room with a thousand walls is cramped.
A man can't take two steps
without running into a corner.
He feels assaulted by tongues
of peeling plaster, dry chips
and a fine white dust sifting
through the wool any room
makes of time and traffic.

A man loses his hand in the jungle
of the top drawer of his dresser.
He pulls out glossy pages
stiff with semen.
The legs of sex.
Glistening organs for sale
like fruit in pint boxes
exposed through plastic net.

Disguised as a child, a twenty-four-year-old model,
partially clothed and provocative
poses in Buster Brown shoes and ankle socks
for *Penthouse*. Above her white pleated skirt
the nipples of her bare breasts are red cinnamon hearts.

A man opens a magazine and enters
the steaming and ruthless
rainforest of his origins.
Something dry and slithering
coils and squeezes out
every other thought.
He flips through pages and grows
a third and murderous arm.
He did not kill the pianist,
like the character in a late-night
horror movie on TV
who borrows hands and talent
to perform in concerts
for an audience attentive
in white linen, pearls, and furs.

There's appetite and then there's hunger.
(I want to understand
this man without grafting
his hands onto my own.)
Bob Guccione didn't intend
his magazine for the man
in a sweat-shop on Spadina.
Even a work-horse knows that much
as he barters with his boss for the remnants
of light through basement windows
barred as if life itself
were a prison sentence
and weather gleaned from the passing
feet he follows from his caged view.

In some stranger's boots he imagines
returning to a home filled with bitching
or laughter, discovering his arms
abundant with the warmth and clean laundry smells
of a wife. Through her soft shirt he can feel
the three tiny hooks holding up her bra.

No, those magazines were designed for men
who are bored with this.

*

Sunday in the freezing rain,
March with its stranglehold on light,
a sun more intimate,
more chilling. A child, a girl
lingering in the park,
rubber boots squeaking,
kicking soft spots in the ice
with her heels.

Lured by her pleated skirt,
lured by the light
of her shiny black boots,
by her soft brown eyes,
turned inward and brooding,
he approaches where Sibelius and the blinds
of rooming-house windows
are the only witnesses.

A man with large hands
and dry, unblinking eyes.

Hypnotized by his stare,
unable to gather even an idea
of escape,
lips quivering in the nightmare,
she silently calls to her mother.

If only he would look away
and break the spell
so she could wake up
and stop herself
from being pulled along.
Where?

*

Breathless in plastic wrap:

she is dressed for outdoors
in the pleated skirt

her mother gave her for Christmas.
And in a brown sweater, its bulky knit
camouflaging her sex,
breasts a boy might have,
tender breasts,
pink and sweet as cinnamon hearts.

In a fridge, like a foetus folded
into that white space
where all dreams end
where she has been made to be
of man unborn.

Note: 'Hunger' is a fiction, based on a composite of persons and events.
The quotation contained in the parenthetical note introducing the poem
was taken from the *Toronto Star*; the forgiveness of the Mennonite parents
of a girl kidnapped and killed in Manitoba.

1986

Orchids and Blood

What do I know of Assam, except that the leaves,
gathered for tea, compose the body of infusions
I savour as Irish breakfast, reading a mystery

or this morning's paper with its massacres
in the Moslem villages:
tribesmen armed with scythes,
a grisly harvest,
children in the fields
naked as grain.

How is tenderness?
Merciless as the creased eyes
in the photograph of a boy
divorced from his father's pocket.
The sun burnishing his curls
like a maid in the morning with cloth
and some miraculous golden oil
blisters and burns everything black
by the afternoon. In Assam, it is not politic
to smell like a meat-eater, to take a bigger plot

of land. Dead bodies pollute the waterholes.
Some were lucky. Some were bent over tasks
and became deaf to the cries it is said
even vegetables make when plucked.
The children like so many ears
of wheat, shredded by storm.

Nothing human is left for a wake.
Cats mourn as they clean the bones,
mourn for milk dried in the breasts
of the mothers they devour.

Homes flame as offerings,
something like prayers for the deceased,
the way killers forgive their victims.

A woman who escapes finds herself
like fruit peeled but uneaten.
She rusts. Her sweetness is wasted.

Some believe that a full moon or a monsoon
or insufferable heat can make us forget
our minds, move to the promptings
of tides and minerals in our blood
in the same way as women menstruate
with the lunar cycle,
in the way they are known to fall
in sync with the rhythms of sisters
and friends. Where love is the bond,
blood is an image of life.

For two years I've balked at the smudge
of printer's ink,
lenten ashes on my fingers.
As if reading about atrocities
precipitates the events.

Giving birth to a child has put me
in the hothouse with Nero Wolfe,
seeking solutions to murder
philosophical and aesthetic.
Dangling among the orchids.

1986

ROBYN SARAH
b. 1949

C Major Scale, Ascending

Nodding off in the brightness of the morning after. Sun
reflects off a neighbour's window, a warm square on scuffed
floorboards, wavering suddenly as the window is opened (the
glass sheet trembling in its cold frame) with just such a
movement as the heart makes when it comes to itself . . .

For a second one imagines opening one's eyes under water, the
moment of adjustment to a new kind of vision, it's all part of
the same phenomenon, coming out of the womb of early
motherhood with a sudden passion for objectivity and a readiness
to try on new voices, like one's own mother's collection of
small silk scarves in a drawer with tangled jewelry and vestiges
of cologne

Always such moments transcend the time of year or day, but the
sun is a constant, the surprise of it, framing some realization,
highlighting the arbitrary: a scrap of paper on the floor, inked
with the words 'C major Scale, Ascending'—left over from a
college course in harmony but seeming suddenly to embody the
whole of what we can know—

Like the smells of bleach and floorwax, one's grandmother
dusting the piano from bass to treble in a series of minor
seconds, there is this music of chance, for which one learns to
compose oneself, a hand in an upstairs window is glimpsed
pouring coffee from a metal pot, or wind turns an umbrella
inside out and everything is ready to begin again, sun breaks
suddenly on the floor like a dropped egg

1984

Study in Latex Semi-Gloss

There is nothing new. Does that matter? Somewhere a woman
is painting her rooms. She had tied up her hair and covered it
with a tattered diaper. Alone, in a flat lit by bare bulbs, she

moves from room to room, her sandals sticking to the spread pages of old Gazettes pooled with paint spills. She is looking for something, for a screwdriver with a yellow handle, with which she nows pries off the lid of the last can of paint; she is stirring the paint with a wooden stick, stirring it longer than necessary, as if it were batter. Now she pours creamy fold upon fold into the crusted tray. The telephone shrills in another room; it is you, but she won't get there in time to answer. If she did, what could you say that would apply here?

Late into the night bare windows frame her, bending and stretching, wielding the roller on its broomstick. Paint streaks her bare arms and legs; some hairs have escaped the cloth about her head to fall in her eyes, and she pushes them aside with the clean back of her hand. In the alley behind the flat, cats couple with strangled yells. Soon she will shut herself in the tiny bath, blinking at the dazzle which dulls the fixtures to the colour of stained teeth; she will tack a torn towel over the window and drop her clothes—the loose jersey with the sleeves cut off, the frayed corduroy shorts, stiff with spatters of paint, at whose edges bunches of dark thread dangle. The underpants, damp and musky with sweat, will fall limp to her ankles. She will squat in the narrow tub, scrubbing at her skin with washcloth, solvent, fingernails, and after, with the cracked remnant of a bar of green soap which she tries in vain to work into a lather. Rinsing with splashed water, she'll pause and hug her knees, hug in the sag of her tired breasts, then stand, stretch, and dry with the clean side of a damp towel. On the toilet she'll bend to examine a broken toenail and remain bent, dreaming, staring at the yellowed tiles.

You will have been asleep an hour, by the time she kills the lights and slips naked into a sleeping-bag spread across a bare mattress on the bare floor. The smell of the bag is the smell of woodsmoke and pine, faint, mixed with old sweat. Perhaps it's the smell that makes her smile a little as she feels herself sucked down into the whirlpool of sleep. Somewhere across blocks and blocks of tenements, her children, half-grown, long limbed, sprawling on foam mats in their father's studio apartment, will stir as a lone car guns its engine in the empty street. She dreams, if she dreams at all, of holes in the plaster, of places where the baseboard is missing, of the bulging and cracking of imperfect surfaces. Dreams the geography of a wall.

There is nothing new. Even what could bloom between you, if you let it, if she let it, goes on as the paint goes on, over old seams, old sutures. Weathers as the paint will weather, flaking along old stress lines. This matters. Think, before you dial again.

What have you to do with those children, blinking sleep from their eyes, breakfasting with their father in a booth of the local diner; where will you be when daylight, like cold water, shocks her awake to pull on yesterday's clothes and squat in the kitchen doorway with her mug of instant coffee? Where, when her clear eyes, steady in their purpose, scan the new surface to discover her painter's holidays?

1984

To Fill a Life

To fill a life as fitful sky fills windows, or a painter, canvas, to fill it willfully, to make large movements within a frame, I think is to be desired—the frame, too, not to contain, but to provoke such movement. No mirror will show you the lines worry pushes your face into, for in the looking, curiosity makes other lines. I want to move far enough away to see you whole, as a child will in a loop that he makes of finger and thumb. *Look how small I can make you, Mummy.*

So the unmade beds of children. So the hats, scarves, mitts, thrown pell-mell over the radiator, so the smell of damp wool filling the hall as the heat rises. On the counter, the jagged shells of breakfast eggs, a crust of stuck whites like brown lace in the cast iron skillet still warm on the burner. So the towels on the bathroom floor, the steamed mirror, stray hairs in the tub and a blue worm of dried toothpaste on the edge of the sink. The tap dripping, humid air smelling of shampoo. The face of a life in motion. The pegs on the rack by the door, on which are slung umbrellas, shawls, soft bags of cloth and leather, the straps wound round each other.

To delight in the weathered, more than in polished planes, to prefer the visible repair to the thing re-done, I think is to respect tenancy, its wear and tear, its fixed term. For each grey hair he pulls from her head, she gives her youngest son a penny, until there are so many, he makes a bankrupt of her, no more, she throws up her hands, laughing. Decades later, when she sells the old house, he comes at night and removes from its hinges the door to the back shed, into whose reluctant grain he and his brothers gouged their names and a date, in boyhood. He puts it on his car, he drives it home and stores it under his stairs. Three names on an unhinged door, the first, of a man dead these twenty-two years. All winter, snow blows into the old shed.

To fill a life. To fill one's own shoes, and walk in them till the plies of the soles begin to separate, till the heels are rubbed away, till the toes turn up and the lettering inside has all flaked off. As fitful sky. To go with the drift of things, shifts of the light and weather. Snow blows into the tracks my skis made this morning: erase all that. I am walking on the face of winter. It's like magic, it's like walking on water, it *is* walking on water. Are you listening? I know a man who photographs the bumps on faces, the tiny lines, who celebrates them with his sharpest focus. I know a man who broke his hammer trying to open a window. Each winter new cracks open in the chimney wall, air currents trace fresh strata of soot across the ceiling.

A pulling against the grain. Amoebas of light in the undulation of gauze curtains, the cross and mesh of lines. Water's resistance as the oars reverse direction. Walking upwind. Syncopation, in music, or certain kinds of dissonance. Cloth cut on the bias, hair combed up from the nape. Velvet, rubbed the wrong way with a finger. Or finger and thumb, cleansed to an edge, testing each other's raised grain. Feeling the lines that frame us, whorl and loop, for life, beyond confusion.

I want to move far enough away to see you whole, I want a lens to contain you, even upside down, as a handful of cast type contains its own impression. As winter contains spring, or the residue of snow, the shape of those things it melted around. The broken tricycle, the rusted spade. It is spring, the season for construction; no backward look in the way that old house is gutted for renovation. I watch from across the street, chunks of my life knocked out like bad teeth, the plaster-dust drifting down like a chalky pall over the gardens. Erase all that. Are you listening?

The face of a life in motion. The sound of pianos out of open windows; radios playing to empty kitchens. On the cold sidewalk, a ring of footsteps: that sound nearly forgotten. Clotheslines shrilling on rusty pulleys; the squeak of baby-carriage wheels. Or close your eyes and it's June, pages torn from a child's copy-book are blowing down the street. In the park, by the stone pond, a line of figures in loose clothing practise Tai Chi, their movements sweeping, rhythmical, echoing each other like the arches of the pavilion behind them, reflected in the water. It's early morning. The movements are large, are generous, they flow, and the clothing too as it fills with wind, flapping against the bodies held there in marvelous postures against the light.

1987

SKYROS BRUCE
b. 1950

From *Kalala*

ONE

when the outside is completely dark
and the room is within itself
shadows adjust.
the tree alone which is
a beautiful growth of the sand
yields to the sun.
houses are marks, black
against the soil.
poor man
in love
and unity—
he is not
even as the blades of grass
imprint on his body
he is not
the shells
the tide
i am not the moon
though worlds revolve
within me
and shadows adjust
to the dark

TWENTY ONE   HOMESICK IN THE CARIBOO

This is a cold, hard
Unfriendly
Land
With natural beauty
So unchanged by civilized manners
It doesn't invite—
(The lakes
With uncatchable colours
More sincere
Then aquamarine
More beautiful   I think
Than the changing of colours
In any land—
Are cold, swift, discouraging
And the highways
Running over the mountains
Are a hurried passport
From the land
Get out
Get out!
The dust
Like a slap in the face
The sage brush
To scratch your legs
This land does everything
To keep you from staying
If you beat it
You won't love it
You'll move on
It's like a prostitute

Now I've had my fill
I saw a face from the dead
And I walked barefoot
In the dust

The tears fell
As pain comes from cancer
You never know till then
The horrors living

Inside of you.
Land of the dead
Day long funeral
Wind blown fresh flowers
On distant graves
In nowhere land
I love the city
Closed in like me
Taking all
But admitting
Slightly committing
Only a few
Who love

TWENTY FIVE

the hay in your womb has turned

to meat and the flesh of your eyes

has denied the right, the flutter down

against your heart

the seed that you wear

around your neck is clear

and cut

because to fly is to be without

except for the makings of the mind

you revolved once in the form of embryo

yourself

and he has heard the songs of your thighs

while you curled against

his scrotum breathing

the prayers that never

ever existed   for you

sure, in spiderdown moors you felt

the web of his semen spring blue

passion into the speechless part

of your mind

the frustration of getting there is in bleeding

all the way back up the womb

and asking your father to set

you free   to be able to love

the way he shot himself instead

of your mother

THIRTY SEVEN

I wanted to tell you, that
when something is pure
it is
        beneath the dove's wing
                        above the iced snow
that is part me part you
and that words come
from the very birds
who make none
and my simple uttering
of the word 'beautiful'
is just
the winds breath
                        in underground tunnels

is just
the boughs acknowledgement of spring
that is,
if you come with your antlers down
you are only hitting the rocks
and there is no need
for the sea   can do that
quite adequately

1972

SUSAN MUSGRAVE
b. 1951

Entrance of the Celebrant

If you could see me,
where I am and where
the forest grows thick and into me;
if you could reach
the darkest centre of myself
and still know the sign of the animal
where it lies apart inside your skin—

then I would say,
that kiss is *my* kiss;
where our lips have touched
were others, and mine are still.

No one forgets
the music of the animal. I've heard
the sound of the old skin cracking
where his heart has become
the heart of something new.
                              If he could see me,
know me, and not forget it was
he who saw me

and that circles tighten and everything
narrows

but that even I am nearing completion,
that everything I have become is something
already gone—

then the dark trees, the sounds
of water across water, of blood
drying still over water—

then his music is the sound of
nobody listening; the animal I carve out
is the shape of darkness, a sound
that nowhere would dare to form.

Animal! Animal!
You are nobody! You cannot be
anyone.

But I had known that
long before your birth

So you died then? Only the dead
can know. My lips revealed you
and my black heart has eaten the hole.
Black fingers pulled a small black night
from between us. Animal, animal
so small are we

that no one wanting
deserves death more.

1972

The Moon Is Upside Down in the Sky

and Paul is in Acapulco
looking for avocados.
Papayas and mangoes are ripening
in the shade; when the moon is this way
we each have hidden powers.

There are frogs in the underworld
singing of the upper air. They
want to go there, they want to
dress in women's bodies and
come to our bed bringing messages
from the spirits.

The bed is cold. Paul is in
Acapulco. Strange beautiful women
are trailing him through the streets—
they know he's not ordinary,
they want to know more about him.

They enter my sleep, like frogs,
like spirit beings; later when I wake
I don't know who I am.
The women are hungry, they wrap
their tongues around me. Their eyes
are the colour of the Acapulco moon,
their skin is like Paul's avocados.

Later we laugh about it, how
Paul was followed home and the bed
filled up with frogs. Still I'm confused;
I think those frogs were human.
Frogs wouldn't look at Paul
that way, like hot-blooded women
in town for a good time.

1985

Cocktails at the Mausoleum

A name may be glorious but death is death
—RICHARD EBERHART

I decided long ago that death
was not serious, if we went
anywhere else it would be less curious.
So I rode into the woods with
an outlaw and his errand-boy
and drank, and made a lot of noise,
at some rich man's mausoleum.

Others had been before, revellers,
to the same place, with little care
for the monument, a vulgar Parthenon.
Of course it was out of place in
those woods, but so were we—
I would have preferred a comfortable bed
but when you ride into the arms
of an outlaw, you lie anywhere.

We lay down together.
I'm afraid the fear had gone out of me,
valuable and available I long ago
had given up my rich husband
preferring to live, if necessary, disreputably.

Here lies so and so I read, turning
my head to breathe the crushed leaves
damp beneath the ghostly boot-heels:
he is dead. I heard ice-cubes clink
in a glass and somebody stirring. You said
there are reasons for death
and proposed a toast to the living.

Oh, it's easy to sniff
but I did not notice when the errand-boy
slipped away, nor my own glass growing empty
while I drank nothing, I was
thinking of love spent, and grief that
gropes slowly like a tendril, gnarled and
clutching over the enormous years.

Here lies so and so, his name
moss-covered though perhaps, to some,
still glorious. I decided long ago
that death was not serious, but now
with a jewelled hand something tugged,
and I felt the cold earth
rising to meet me.

It's no matter. All my life I had been
waiting for a sign, for death, too,
because I was born wanting. *There are
good reasons for death,* you said,

and sucked the spicy liquor from my
last small breath.

1985

'I Do Not Know If Things That Happen Can Be Said to Come to Pass or Only Happen'

but another year has passed
and the change is marked.
Right from the start my life stopped
making sense

at the core there was only terror,
a compass of blood in the heart's
wreckage and blood and more blood
in every direction.

It spilled out of me,
there was no reason.
As a child I buried everything
I loved, buried it down deep
and seemed pleased.

Years later the doctors
dragged it up,
opened me inside and cut the
stubborn mother from my womb.

My father rocked in his chair
unable to share his last breath
with anyone.
That was years ago when we
thought he wouldn't live much longer.
He still drives down the highway
to see me.

Ten years ago I spent Christmas
in a locked ward.
Some of my best friends
had already committed suicide.

I tried too but it wasn't in me.
The terror went deeper
where nothing could reach me.
I fell in love easily
and for no reason.
I still think, even now, I could be
more discriminating.

Another year has passed,
a decade.
Walking on New Year's Day
with friends who have survived
like me, by accident
—there is something to be said
for having such friends—
I think of the choices we made
along the way, how things
came to pass, or happened,
what brings us finally together.

The years will make sense of it.
Deeper into the shadows
where the patient trees endure
and grow, a small bird rises up
out of our silence, crying
shy and wild towards open water.

1985

ROO BORSON
b. 1952

A Sad Device

A rat, his eyes like glycerine,
like galleries of landscape paintings,
genitals like a small bell, he,
siphon of smells,
mortician gathering in the gauzy corpses,
construes the world.
The grey warehouse of gothic stars,

the gleaming artillery of water,
the flowerbeds like Arabic scrolls,
all of it.

I think my heart is a sad device,
like can-openers.
Sometimes I would rather step between slices
of dark rye and be taken in
by some larger beast.
Men dreaming of billboards,
cars barrelling on and on in a night marooned,
zeroed in on an immense target.

Now I believe the frozen mammoths
in the laundry room
came of their own accord,
not through coercion
by the Sears appliance man.
Not even he
has a cozy life.

1981

Jacaranda

Old earth, how she sulks,
dark spin-off
wielding wings and swords,
mountain ranges, centuries,
our eyes with their impurities.

Dusk. Planets like spilled mercury
and the stars exuding
loneliness, the old battle
for which there are no medals.

Often I look in that mirror
in which things happen over again.
Useless. Or I look
to the teasing water full of days
and clouds that drift like smoke,
and hours when the head sleeps,

an inn for strange guests. If only
we were easier creatures.

But the jacaranda reclines
like a wise thing,
stars crystallizing
beyond its dusky plumes.
Here in the amethyst air of early autumn,
the dryness a talisman,
the moon the egg of a luminous bird,
the jacaranda's wand–like branches
command each thing to be.

1981

Blackberries

The eucalyptus shadows hang
like knives, knives that cut nothing,
shadows. A breeze starts up
like a little thrill
going through a crowd. The wet smoke smell.
A shadow shivers over the hills
and the two girls still picking blackberries
down in the bushes stop and listen.
They've been told about this wind. They've been told
it can get you pregnant, that in the dark spaces
between bushes sometimes a man crouches.
That at the sight of a girl a man
just goes crazy, he can't help himself.
They keep picking, but faster. All they want
is some blackberries. Their mothers tell them that someday
they'll get more than they bargained for
staying out this late. They know they should be going.
But the sun leaks out again, dimly,
then floods over the bushes, over their hands and faces,
a heat which turns their skin white again
and sparkles on the leaves. The blackberries
are taut and warm and sweet; the kernels shine
like the thoraxes of solitary ants making their way
across the dirt. The girls have a game
with sunlight, they pretend

it makes them invisible. But around their mouths
and on their fingers the ragged pink stains
will take a long, long time to go away.

1984

Rain

The bay the color of steel, of a warship
with scattered sun and cloud on its flanks,
the color of a battlefield
after it's all over,
of a soldier's mind when there's nothing left to kill,
in the immediate vicinity anyway,
and he can rest
but what is that kind of rest worth?
There's always going to be something left alive.

The water from a tin cup
tastes thin and substanceless,
you can never get enough.
It's not that the first time wakens
a bloodthirst, it's that you cross over
to a country where everything's different,
a country of men
who don't know what they're after.
Everything tastes thin.
You take it all in, trying to get satisfied.
Then you just shut off.

Rain zig-zags down between the hills.
It shatters on rooves, and there are people inside
just sitting around listening.

If you're an ex-soldier you're out walking in the rain,
you're used to it. Hands in pockets,
the sidewalk full of shoes scraping past,
trousers, the bunched hems of dresses under coats.
You look at people from the bottom up.
Sometimes a pair of women's eyes catches
at your throat, at the way it was when you were a kid,
always wanting to know what came next,

like a movie full of possible surprise endings,
which way would it turn out?

But you never expected this. Never thought
the whole thing could just go on and on,
no end in sight, not much happening, just the rain,
the grey sidewalk and the shoes, soggy shoes
filled with other people's lives. The warm women
hurrying beneath their dresses.
Out on the street
you see people in-between things, never
the place they've left or where they're going, only
their faces with that look of expectation.

Except of course for the ones who live out on the street,
who stay there rain or shine, slumped in doorways,
sunk in their own eyes.

Further off the hills are blurred with white mist.
It's coming down hard there too. But from here
it just looks like a white mist that slowly blows and changes.

1984

Flying Low

On the hundred hills
the straw signals in the wind.
Sometimes a whole arc of it shines.

Every family is different, but in each one
they have the same eyes.
Every time they look at one another
there's that mirror.
There's no help for it.

Our family's eyes are the color of mud,
of cliffs, full
of tiny landslides that amount to nothing.
They are the sheen on puddles,
the sun that doesn't see anything better to light up.

Of my two brothers the older is always watching
the younger, and the younger is always going somewhere.
Or he used to be; right now
he's flying us in circles over the hills
where we all grew up. That small cross of shadow
is us, twisting into a bird, a straight line.

Families are all the same. They talk to one another
inside their heads, thinking the others can hear.

The sunset flashes on our faces as we twist away
over the shoreline, over the pale red foam,
but our tiny shadow stays back in the hills, rumpling over them,
over that spot we all know. Long ago
each of us fell and hurt himself
one too many times and opened those eyes
that could have been any one of ours

to his own face reflected in the dirt.

1984

St Francis

For the last weeks the daylight hours have fallen short and shorter.
Transfixed by yellow porchlight to a wicked chartreuse, shadow-
plants spring up all around. Enamel primroses, and snowdrops looking
down like tiny streetlamps from their tall stems. The garden bears its
losses with a quiet we have never accustomed ourselves to: even the
crickets have taken their gypsy music elsewhere.

The little St Francis looks out from his jagged pulpit high on the
cedar trunk, clay birds landing on his clay shoulders. He'd be lost
without them, for they were born that way, joined. Like all saints he
gazes straight ahead at a single point. The black veils of the cedar
boughs shade him, for he is frail, and they live here.

As the youngest, I remember when my father and brothers used
to work outdoors. They'd go halfway around the house just to douse
the crooked ring of cedars under St Francis with their urine. Standing
beside one another or alone they seemed distanced, as if in some
animistic prayer.

But I remember St Francis most for those April dawns when I
was the first awake. The amaryllis siphoned its pinkness from under-

ground springs of cologne. The sun would just touch him and he'd blush as if a woman had come too near, and all day the jays would land and take off again, taunting him like delinquent boys, for he was no bigger than they were.

1984

JAN CONN
b. 1952

All Women Dream of Snakes

All women dream of snakes,
I've been told, Freud in the background—
his reductionist view of sexuality.
Personally, I prefer snakes to men.

It must have a lot to do
with the texture of their skin
(belts, purses, shoes)
and the lack of legs
so every movement is a sort of dance—
grace they slide in and out of
like a hand in a glove.

As for turtles: the standard
pet-shop ones, fed raw hamburger and spinach,
always died within a week,
though once a huge one visited our cottage
and stayed all summer.
We took it for walks,
gave it delicacies
such as bubble gum and string.
It soon learned
to bite the hands that fed it.

With frogs I'm more sympathetic.
Especially a certain Amazonian one
used as poison by the Indians.
One drop of extract from its skin
can kill a small cow.

Whenever I open the slim volume of Bashō
I hear the silence after they've leapt
from lily pad to still deep water.

Late one night coming home on the streetcar,
a boy with a white styrofoam box
told two girls beside him
there was a frog inside,
hoping for admiration, later,
conversation. *They get stranded
in lettuce crates,* he explained.
Same shade of green.

Everyone has a primitive brain.
Only yesterday the baby brontosaurus
curled at the base of my skull
went out for a walk,
dragging me along into the swamp.

I had to wait around while it ate
everything green and slimy in sight.
Feed me, it said. Feed me.

1986

While I Was Looking at the Background You Walked Out of the Picture

I've sent you a tiger. Its fur burns intense orange,
radiant against the dark. Plants around it
send up volleys of smells, fantastic.

Its ears are filled with white hair,
a thousand moth antennae
bent in and listening to dreams
of the rain forest: fat frogs creaking,
a prey of insects crackling.

You leave me behind, always,
coming home months later, from India,
Africa, Colombia—with another

smell on your skin, a suitcase
of saris and ivory elephants for your wife,

and smaller gifts for us, the daughters, growing
like Hallowe'en pumpkins, awkward teeth
stuck in our grins.

I decide to become an archaeologist,
to go where you've been
while the scent is still fresh.

1986

Two Paintings of Lily Pads

One, green on black, stark, precise.
It's midnight on the pond
or the painter emerging
from three days of alcohol
about to be overwhelmed by a hint of pink,
a bud, a woman's sex freeze-framed.

Opposite, pastels immersed
in soap-bubbled light, vague impressions,
the light much as it is now,
late afternoon, diffuse,
so the lily pads are merely
projections of themselves,
underdeveloped negatives.

After dusk, the gravel causeway to Flores
an egret's wing balanced on black water.
The lake's membrane pulled tight
except at the edges, where it riffles—

letting go the trapped gas,
the intricate lives of micro-organisms.
Lily pads undulate,
landing pads for minute spaceships,
origin of these bizarre frogs,
in pairs, like handcuffs,
found nowhere but this lake.

We read about their delicate
nervous system, their mating habits,
a pornography of speckled, iridescent skin.

Their music swells the lavender sky,
breaking in on the painter's sleep.
He rolls over, cursing.
He would like to shoot
the frogs' pale bellies,
watch them splatter the lake.

He would also shoot the moon
for coming into his room uninvited
and making the woman's skin
glow like pearls, like the unprotected
side of a fish.

He pushes his penis into her
to shut out the raucous frogs,
their uninhibited couplings.

1986

JUDITH FITZGERALD
b. 1952

From Diary of Desire

From *February*

RAILROAD ROMANCE

Leaving Montreal as a continuing segment of our railroad romance
as you name it and impart its sense of substance, of subject and
    object
and the reliquary significance we embrace and trace along similar
lines of thought, of longer trains, passages into light and shadows
    and
darknesses and the longer trains, longer life lines with the wheels
spinning on and on.

And to what do I return? Turning to face the window, the glass

fragments, rearranges the landscape of my features in superimposed
apparitions, the shadows of these random houses and fields which
duplicate our eyes, our bodies gliding the necessary trajectory away
from each other, from pure romance and now, looking down
into the St Lawrence River my fingers begin a confused and
    disobedient
language that tears the nails out and ties up communication.

Over. Over the St Lawrence the train held suspended in breath by a
    bridge
spanning my hands making these awkward marks, the Quebec
    landscape
a safescape; the whistle blows three times and I recall mourners'
benches, penitent forms and amen corners, the proximity of my
    mouth
shaping glass on this train while the whistle repeats itself
in the fine, oh so fine, metrical time, encouraging introspection and
desire.

Duomo. Prie-dieu. Missa. I will worship at the station of our love
and ignore the guild and guilt and grace in safety through arrivals
and departures, remember the passion reiterating itself in the
    stuttering
speed of this train between worlds, cultures apart, sometimes *grave,*
sometimes *tempo ordinario,* sometimes *prestissimo:* The forgivable
paces of train travel. Religion does not enter

this travelling, these earth–clinging bodies moving east or west
    telling
the beads of a journey towards the other: I will come and go
and you will come and go and we will become a perfect celebratory
incantation crossing the Ontario-Quebec border. Notice the snow,
the wide fields spread out past our private view of this landscape
shared between us in rest or in motion. Separation.

The whistle will always sound and we will always sound too,
a tone, a third space in orchestration; arrivals and departures and
attention to this hymn in transit sway us. We await destinations,
callings. We travel the borders of night and longing where morning
makes us up and the cold sun brings love to its urgent loss. The
    train
will rattle on and we will gather in these fields of ice and night
and need. We shall isolate ourselves in blankets of desire.

August

HOW DO YOU SPELL RELIEF?

For Hugh Hood

Midnight and the clips manage a manic arrangement
on the screen; somewhere the reenactment of the seventh
inning occurs and occurs and winces in full colour;
the reminder, the replay, the lack of.

And, how do you *spell* relief? Bring in the terminator
from another channel/league, a different wavelength? Bring in the
    ace
stopper (in the hole), watch the left hand's precision unfold slo-
mo terrific? Imagine Willie rising on the right side of a star?

Concentrate. Each wild pitch out of your control as the kite
red sun sets infinitely blue in the moonlight window, hangs
disconsolate while eyes gnaw the heart of a dilemma—
to go beyond and get out of the inning, this game.

Think over plays in fields memorized without originals backing
accurate imagining; the way only Roger Angell can call a season
    dulcet;
the way George Bowering can call a muscle move, a pitch, a game
    before
the action knows its inspiration, cause, effect.

Relief. Heart-hazed soft sun/moon evenings; the stands forgotten
as the bases fill up and grand slams glaze intaglio the superimposed
fields. The go-ahead in the batter's box and here comes the pitch
and it's a swing and a miss. And it doesn't matter. And it does.

THE BASEBALL HALL OF FAME

She had always wanted to play baseball, eight letters, an octave
of motion. So when she started driving taxi for a living
she tuned the radio to the ballgame and turned the car down
Toronto streets. Toronto grew up, grew old, grew older.
Old enough to move up to the majors. Not keys, but leagues.
Minor leaves fluttered through webs of memory in oldtimer's
mouths. *Sunnyside. Hanlan's Point. Babe Ruth.* She knew
the stories. The volume. Statistics erupted.

She always wanted to play baseball so when she drove
the taxi she said she wouldn't unless it turned out it
had a radio, AM, she said. That's the kind of girl I am.
Ain't touching no car without a radio.
And she didn't.

And when she went to the park and when it rained. Sun would
    shine
but she would find a pocket of rain and zip it up. Stands
smelling of memories. Jackson and Cobb and Chapman and
FitzGerald and *tell Carl it's okay*. She just wants to play.

The mound. Eyes following the line to the mound and Venus,
she thought Venus, invariably, and wanting, always wanting to
play, she|thought|inches, feet. Ninety feet. Nightly rituals.
Daily desires. She undressed to the national anthem. Waning.
She couldn't see the lights.

She never made the majors. She wound up and let a slow
curve continue until it covered the field, the line,
the composition. She always wanted to play baseball
but baseball had a heart of its own. She stuffed the mitt
in the backseat window and picked up low stations
and milked the meter and went to the games.

She wanted to play baseball and when the Blue Jays came
to town she painted it red. Some sense to the chaos of driving.
Slick city now: Car wielding fenders and carburetors and pistons
and alternators. A lot of horsepower. Slant six. Ball four. Fury.
Took a lot to warm it up but she cruised by hitters and they never
came close to her change-up. Her over. Her out.

She wanted to play. Spent years gently creasing pages
of southpaw dreams, scratches of sweet sliding heavenly bodies.
Everything forgotten. The time, place, space. A question
of physics. She had the positions down. Watched the 1-6-4
and knew.

She carried bits of mythology in worn pockets and scribbled new
    stats
she studied under moon. Stitched craters. Hovering over the plate.
That kindness of protection.

But she wanted, needed, desired and eventually she did. Became
the game and each team the moment she played hard. Hard ball.
Hard hitter. Straight shooter. And clichés grew around her night
vision, mare, her *sea of heartbreak,* her moon over heartache.

She mounted a sea of taxi and let loose. Curved down thruways
and lanes and crescents and highways and ain't it a bitch? Late, late
and street-empty she rode the crest of the Avenue Road hill
    watching
taxis float ghostly down to Davenport, swans, similes carved in
    wheels.

She had Clancy and she had Fernandez and she had McLain and she
    had
sweet bugger all. That's what happened. That's what hit her. She
    jumped.
Drove off to the northwest and set up shop in marriage. Said yes, I
    do,
I do too. Picked up a sucker and made him her own. Guy never
    knew the score.

So she always and after she packed in the taxi and retired
the glove and took her a husband, she found some sort of uneasy
alliance, some little-league consolation in cooking tired bacon and
    eggs
and remembering *easy over, strike three, you're out.*

And forgetting the grand slam.

AUGUST EVENINGS

Moving pictures again. Cruising Yonge Street
Friday full-moon night and pavement sweats women.
Hot, damp, early. Girls until dawn, madams of matter, ladies of
    love.

Slow curves. Languid against bright reflections in the window
of Ford Drugs between johns and tricks and mirrors
and does and doesn't matter.

What could she say? Desire doesn't give
an inch, a damn, a second glance. Human
intercourse. Prime numbers in the shade.

A left-handed love in a right-handed glove.
The race goes on and these words curl
in an intersection of wounds.

LINE DRIVES

Heart held in the glove of abeyance, suspended animation, so much
the space of need in the shape of love. Little things. *Do wah diddy.*
The way your smile breaks the barrier reef of this porcelain
    madness.
The ubiquitous hit parade, made less magical than necessary, more
    romantic
than possible. *Met him on a Monday and my heart stood still.* Till
    Friday.
Moon comes down to kiss water, throws a life line of heart to save
    this drowning image.
Need of another, desire of desire, the end of innocence signals the
    thread of regret,
weaves the night eccentric. Slides romance between the leaves of
    love.

Baseball, I desert you against my best intentions, deny your
    stunning
order, lack of chaos, prayer of perfection. Such beauty I cannot
    bear.

1987

CAROLYN SMART
b. 1952

Telling Lies

Drugged with light, the lack of it
or longing, she stays on later than she thought,
charmed by streets familiar with you,
any building haunted by surprising grace,
nostalgia's dusk or autumn, but it's later than that:
she's just waiting for the sight of you

Who wants to hear this,
her wanting you, being tired of it,

the smell of traffic from other lives,
her so static, therefore lying
about anything, whatever holds back loss:
a memory, the narcotic you have become

Her stiff with denial and silence,
drinking it dull in the shade or breeze,
drunk and alone saying to the dream
Shut up   Come in off these mazy streets
It is only one more world's end lying,
her believing in measureless, fantastic light

A frivolous heart beating once, twice, erratic,
shocked by dependence on you, this need she has
for the sight of you, sound of your voice,
always her watching, windows with their dusty stare,
the dark outside and no-one awake to listen:
she's telling lies, truth's a phantom only visible at night.

1986

Flying

For Mary di Michele

All our lives they've said we expect too much
from what bone and the spark of cells
will make of a simple life
Two of us so eager for the future we imagine
we smoke the air for speed
anything to get what we want   perfection
Believe we can change the world
with language   a tool to call down the stars
watch them come   eager puppies   to the page
You and I are reckless
wanting to believe in everything
a planet of kindness

Your hand on my arm at a party
touches beyond our public selves
past false conversation   clink of glass on wood
stories people tell about their lives
later thinking *why did I say so much*

who will hurt me
but your hand is saying to me
care imagine believe
touching the way women touch each other
for comfort for rest
This from your small hand trust
the world we desire

For your birthday I give you a gathering of friends
never expecting the gift you will give
Not knowing you change me forever you say
once everybody could fly
bright eyes arms in the air as you talk
saying this perhaps for the first time
with such ease my eyes fill up
relief of shared vision
You a small child clinging to steep rock
head already part of the sky
holding on so tight because you know
with only one brief gesture you could fly
without even trying floating
only a step away not surprised by this
not afraid your concern only for your mother nearby
who has forgotten all she knew about flight
knows terror you hold onto the earth
choose this still believe
Once you say to us *everybody could fly*

Then you sit back hands still face glowing
Four other voices remember dreams and Peter Pan
I could have said
waiting for the light to change
the steering-wheel solid in my hands
I saw trees about to burst open
clouds moving too fast above the city
and then I knew what I'd always known
if I just let go the air would take me
I thought I was at the edge of madness
felt the sky pulling and thought it wanted my soul
knew it would be so easy but I held on

I could have said
again and again it happens

I feel the speed of the planet
as it rolls through space   such silence
the ground under my feet gives up gravity
clouds begin their whirl
I know this all so well   one more step
and I would be flying

My deepest secret
fear always in the telling
what if they banished me   put me away
like children with golden eyes who practise levitation
some kind of science-fiction or madness
the terror of misunderstanding
You have taken the loneliness of silence from me
with your need to believe
in what this world could be

Bone and the spark of cells
is all we have ever had
We see so clearly what we want
from a simple life
Language and touch bring us closer
to what we once knew before fear
The belief in tenderness   innocence
Remember   one more step and then
the air

1986

KATE VAN DUSEN
b. 1952

Valentime

no time like the
no time anymore I like you
or me. it stops when we say

(but I can't) goodnight.
BMW whizzes away. I'm left with
Union Station. and a pounding
not hard

to tear yours out
in a minute. would never stitch
it tho she does
her expensive magic.

on last night's news:
4 hours from start to finish!
his dark fingers work fast.
saves nine. he saves

lives. works precisely
around the red thumping
thing. the irreplaceable
machine.

when he's done they play
Mozart! yours I'd tear
out in a moment. moment
of frozen rage on Queen St.

leather mini and junked out
eyes! 'lets get a closer look!
may as well get her to read
in the series.' so big

and yet such a little
lump of mind
lessness. back home
to a black house

and the power out: an old
slow anger at power
lessness. the whole harbour
the frozen lump
of my heart. irreplaceable
machine. broken by some big
thug. thumping his way
nowhere near to me.

leaving a bay full
of frozen rage. in my pocket
a dull ticking. time

thumping by. it will soon
be all over. all of this
n'iceness.

1987

For Me and Me

and spring too has its audacity.
pushes its yellow blooms against
the cracked glass of my windows.

insists on another postcard
of turquoise blue sky. insists
in fact on any number of gorgeous
contrasts to what this is.

the young know this. jump off
bridges in their tight black jeans
and smash up their father's cars
like decent folk.

but there will be other springs
will there not be Father? (O pray
say yes for indeed we come back
to you and your fluffy truths
when we are in need.)

at thirty-two the little electric
wire comes; the quick knowing
that in the fragrant air
there is nothing but death.

too many ghosts here. of the living
as well as dead. and they won't be
any fewer. the spring

has its audacity and I have mine
sitting here in red t-shirt
complaining about the brilliance.
the minute illumination

of every detail of blossom
and the unbearable blue of sky.
while you are not sitting here.
and will not be sitting here.

nor ever will be. nor will he.

I sit and complain about having
no one to write for anymore.
and write more and more
for me and me.

1987

Not Noir

For Dorothy & me

November arrives, a strolling horror
with a dry voice. without even
a trace of the tingling
expectations the sisters at Elsinore had.

The room crackles with absence.

Miss Havisham wears black lace.
is a tattered negative of herself
pouring out two glasses
of cheap champagne.

Drinking one of them
while she performs
that specialty of women.
waiting
for the guest who will not
show up.

And the unabashed human heart
will stupidly search for a glimmer
in even this in even this grim
dark.

Blow out the candles now.
pull the plug from the electric
alphabet.

If there is a word
for this mood this night
it is not *noir*
but utterly unredeemable

black.

1987

DIONNE BRAND
b. 1953

Amelia

I know that lying there in that bed
in that room
smelling of wet coconut fibres
and children's urine
bundled up in a mound
under the pink chenille and cold
sweating sheets
you wanted to escape,
run from that room
and children huddling against you
with the rain falling outside
and flies and mud
and a criminal for a son
and the scent of the sewer heightened
by the rain falling.
on those days
she tried to roll herself
into the tiniest of balls on the bed
on those days she did not succeed
except in turning the bed into a ship
and she, the stranded one
in that sea of a room
floating and dipping
into the waves, the swell

of a life anchored.
I think that she would have been better
by the sea
in the guayguayare,
but in the town
hot with neighbours and want
she withered and swelled
and died and left me
after years of hiding
and finally her feet fearful and nervous
could not step on asphalt
or find a pair of shoes.
swimming in the brutish rain
at once she lost her voice
since all of its words contained her downfall.
she gargled instead the coarse water from her eyes
the incessant nights
the crickets call
and the drooping tree,
breathed, in gasps
what was left in the air
after husband and two generations of children.
lying in a hospital bed
you could not live by then
without the contradictions
of your own aggrieved room
with only me to describe the parking lot outside
and your promise, impossible,
to buy me a bicycle,
when they brought your body home
I smiled a child's smile of conspiracy
and kissed your face.

1984

Amelia continued . . .

1. I leave everyone on roads
   I linger until I am late
   I mistake bedrooms for places where people sleep
   I scratch letters on mud slides,
   of late I am called a mule

not for my hard headedness
but for my abstentious womb.

2. I am in love with an old woman
    who bequeathed me a sentence or two
    'don't grow up and wash any man's pants,
    not even out of kindness'
    this, and a bit of spittle
    wrapped in an old newspaper.

3. now
    I forget
    hemmed in by sieges and military occupations
    languages
    I forget the country
    I forget myself and wave and smile
    against the twentieth century.

4. Presently I have a vile disposition
    it does not appreciate great sunsets
    from 'the villa' looking over the carenage,
    old fort and point salines
    not even the afternoon sun
    escapes my criticism.

1984

Diary—The grenada crisis

In the five a.m. dusk
grains of night's black drizzle, first stones
boulders of dark
sprinkle the open face
open eyes, incense of furtive moths
badluck's cricket brown to the ceiling
I am watching two people sleep.

in the morning smoke light
my chest and its arms cover my breasts,
the ground, wet, the night before,
soil scented,
the open vault of the morning,

scented as the beginning and end of everything
after a while, villainy fingers the eyes,
daubs the hills disenchant
and the mouth lies in its roof
like a cold snake.

coals lit
and contained in clay, glowing
a horizon like a morning coal pot,
still an old woman stooping—cold
churches coral their walls on the ridge,
I could exchange this caribbean
for a good night's sleep
or a street without young men.

the ghost of a thin woman
drifts against the rim of the street,
I thought nothing was passing,
in the grey light before the crying animals,
when I saw her dress and her pointed face,
I am climbing the steps to the garbage dump,
a woman frightens me.

In the pale air overlooking the town
in the anxious dock
where sweat and arms are lost
already,
the ship and the cement
drop against the metal skies,
a yankee paratrooper strangles in his sheet.

prayers for rain,
instead again this wonderful sky;
an evening of the war and those of us looking
with our mouths open
see beauty become appalling,
sunset, breaths of grey clouds streaked red,
we are watching a house burn.

All afternoon and all night,
each night we watch a different
fire burn,
Tuesday, Butler House

Wednesday, Radio Free Grenada
Thursday, The Police Station
A voice at the window looking
'the whole damn town should burn'
another 'no too many of us will die'.

eyes full of sleep lie awake
we have difficulty eating,
'what's that' to every new sound
of the war.

In the five a.m. cold light
something is missing,
some part of the body, some
area of the world, an island,
a place to think about,

I am walking on the rock of
a beach in Barbados
looking to where Grenada was
now, the flight of an american bomber
leaves the mark of a rapist in the room.

of every waking,
what must we do today,
be defiant or lie in the
corridor waiting for them,
fear keeps us awake
and makes us long for sleep.

In my chest,
a green-water well,
it is 5 a.m. and I
have slept with my glasses on
in case we must run.

the last evening,
the dock and the sky make one,
somewhere, it has disappeared,
the hard sky sends
military transports,
the darkness and my shoulders

meet at the neck,
no air comes up,
we have breathed the last of it.

In the Grand Etang
mist and damp
the road to Fedon
fern, sturdy,
hesitate
awaiting guerrillas.

1984

SUSAN GLICKMAN
b. 1953

America

Whatever else it is,
it's big. It travels under its own steam,
barrelling down the rails to that vanishing point
where all the tracks converge.
Grasses littered with cornflowers, sweet William, daisies,
surge out of its path, murmuring
like the sea, or the sighs of an audience
before the curtain rises on a deft third act
where everything will be resolved.
Meanwhile, Act II.
A family comes in to breakfast,
immigrant parents and half-grown sons.
The last trace of dreams still blurring their eyes
they greet each other warily,
groping across the table with a few words, fossils
from the old country.
These are boys who buckle their belts tightly.
They always make two sandwiches for lunch:
salami and cheese pasted together
with mayonnaise or mustard, a damp frill
of lettuce. They eat deliberately, both hands clamped on the bread,
looking at nothing, or at girls who are next to nothing,
advertisements for romance in black leather
to pose pillion on motorcycles

the boys imagine riding
across America.

1986

Families

Once at the breakfast table when that harsh bitching
that passes for a stab but is really more like sawing away
with a rusty breadknife, leaving a jaggedy scar,
passed as usual in those days between my mother
and me my father began to cry
into his cornflakes. Big round tears for the lost family
on the cereal box; the one that was supposed to come
with the yellow breakfast nook, the apple tree
out back. Only one tree, our neighbour's, dropping its fruit
over the fence. Generous, but not big enough
to hide in, so there was nowhere to shelter, no option
but escape. But Dad had his job, his car, his sense of humour;
deep down hadn't he always known there *was*
nowhere else to go? That a family only keeps smiling
in photographs and even there
someone's always out of focus. Him, for example;
his eyes inevitably shut, as though caught by chance
between blinks, when really, it was a reflex, like sneezing.
He could smile or keep his eyes open—but not both.

I could make that a metaphor I guess, or quote Tolstoy in
Anna Karenina, but happiness in families is also complex
and not to be sneezed at. The problem is more with the way
we apprehend feelings in time. Sadness is so slow, a mule with
split hooves, picking its way over stone. Joy,
in this ratio, a 40's convertible, his first car,
speeding down green summer roads to a *doo-wap* refrain.
That is, when you're happy you don't have to know all the words,
humming along does just fine. But grief,
grief makes us all precisions, analyzing each other
to death: *you failed me, and this is exactly how*.

Meanwhile the evidence of our honourable if partial success
piles up—all those turkeys, ribbons, pots of flowers.
In their albums the smiles brave out our disregard,
bleaching a little with the years like the cedar dock down

at the lake, that worn path between the house
and the silent water: between what contains the family
and what it keeps them from. Lying on that dock with eyes closed
I told my mother all about you before we were married,
when I still wasn't sure; some of the old harshness in my voice
because I wanted or expected her to tell me not
to do it, to tell me the pains were more real
than the joy. But she didn't. No one could save me from my own
trip down that road; no one wanted to.
And so I jumped off the split grey boards into the reflections
of trees and clouds and swam away very fast from that house
to this one, into a new family. Eyes wide open,
but under water.

1987

Who's There?

Where does the room go
when the lights go out?
The chairs, the blank wooden face
of the table close in
on themselves, into the secret life
of things which our life,
fitfully, interrupts.

I know this.
Crossed wires, especially
in spring; there is this
other life.
It's the same with the mountain, in snow or sun;
the same with the grey lake
by the grace of whose true creatures
I am permitted to explore.

See how carefully I swim?
Displacing very little water,
almost a fish, really;
quite recently a fish.

It is only parents who believe anyone
can be protected.
After all, that's their job.

Footsteps.
Now they are coming closer.
Now they are going away.

1987

JANICE KULYK KEEFER
b. 1953

My Mother, a Closet Full of Dresses

In Poland, needing a dress
for the potato masher to become a doll,
she cut out a patch from somebody's
Sunday skirt—black silk, good enough
to be buried in; waterfalling folds—
no one would notice. Before the whole church,
Baba bent to kiss the icons; her skirts
fanned, the missing patch a window
to her starched white drawers.
My mother whipped until she could not sit;
the baba never setting foot
in church again.

In Canada, her sewing teacher
called it shameful—a girl of such gifts
entering a factory! Sent her
to design school instead, dressed
in her castoffs. My mother, slashing
stitches from priggish Liberty prints—
everyone else flaunting
palm leaves, cabbage roses.

The Story of a Dress at the Exhibition.
She sat in a small display-cage, designing,
cutting out, sewing a dress.
The man who grilled her on each
click of the scissors, till she bit
blistered lips, blood
drooling down her chin.
Watched for a week,
then hired her like that—

though it was still Depression,
designers a dime a dozen.

The wedding dress she sketched
and sewed herself: 'The bride in peau de soie
with a delicate rose tint and beading
in the shape of scattered leaves.'
Satin peignoirs from the honeymoon—
tea-coloured stains; folds creased
as with a knife.

A closet full of dresses for weddings,
anniversaries,
funerals—

And occasions for which she didn't dress:
children with high fevers, and husband
off playing golf or bridge as husbands did;
the miscarriage when she bled
faster than the ambulance; migraines
in dark rooms at noon;
and all the nights
when she rummaged, naked,
through steel hangers in an empty closet.

1986

Late Show

Nightbound in this sleeping house
somebody cries; though the television's
been left on, tears re-run,
re-run. There is an etiquette of dreams,
you don't just walk into another person's head
without knocking.

Her eyelids a blackboard
chalked with barnyard animals.
Fourteen, and sent to kindergarten
to learn English. When he taps
the rooster she can name
in Polish, Ukrainian, Russian, she says

'Chicken's Father.' Children laugh
as his ruler splits her palm.

For playing hockey instead of violin
he has been beaten; locked
in his room, his bow carving scales
up and down his arm
as his sisters grate beets
in the cellar.

Downstairs, her chair and his
in separate corners, opposite a screen
jagged with interference: storms
blistering from dreams.

1986

Children's Drawings on the Theme of Peace

Papers stuck against the walls
like bits of bandage over seeping wounds:
pictures of peace; by default, war—
Siamese twins, unseverable, schizoid.

On this side hands lopped at the wrist
signalling Victory; doves like ducks
frenzied by hunters' bullets. Here,
butterflies big as bombers, dodging
scrawny rainbows: there, stick-figures
joining fractured arms. Not images of peace:
signs of war's absence.

Across the hall, bright horrors
learned by rote. Symbols
phosphorescent with half-life:
poppies still bleed in Flanders Fields;
swastikas limp—amputee spiders.
Ivan the Terrible and G.I. Joe
drop huge, acutely detailed bayonets
to shake the rudiments of hands,
and one diminutive 'atomike bombe'
like a bad boy, in a corner—

as if the atom were some Humpty-Dumpty
happily untoppled on his wall.

On every page the same dead signs
—except for this: one bare brick wall,
a finger's breadth of sky.
Over the wall, two eyes,
stick arm, a small white flag;

traces of birds—
too far away to tell
if they are scavengers or doves.

1986

Perceptual Elegy

Out a bare window I watch darkness
snatching at the garden. Days of small rain
have cleared the streets, but here
no change—still winter squatting
on the cusp of spring. Branches withhold buds
as cross children, kisses; starlings
gurgle on brittle stalks—darkling, I listen
but there is no cue. Loose light,
dun grass, small deaths discovered
by retracting snows.

This room blackens with the garden—slow,
sensory *Liebestod*. With you
I'd garden darkness, we would play
each other the way wind does those fir trees,
blurring the needles' edge.
Unseen, invisible, apart—I crave
the glazier's skill, spreading glass
between air and air, cementing
two transparencies;

perform analogy instead, turning
birch into our long legs,

intertangled—the scar-pink
under sloughing bark, our skin

feeding on looks and likenesses
till night undoes eyes
and what they hold. Black,
being no colour, kills by stealth
—the birch and I
columns of ash, dispersing in the dark,
both sides of the glass.

1986

RHEA TREGEBOV
b. 1953

Reflected Light

We have to pretend we don't know it's
happening—the wall pushing at the earth,
the earth pushing just as fiercely back;
the wall flung round wide in circles like
a yo-yo at the end of its string, tethered
but wobbling inwards; falling slowly from
nothing into nothing—scientific fact.

I know it because I see it; stacked up on
itself stone by stone it's giving itself
up, being peeled back through a history of
paint, plaster, cream, terra-cotta, pink;
a thick red line fading in and out to frame
the window.

I know it because I see it, reflected light,
because this is all the world available to
us. The chance of clear sunlight has me
absorbed in this vision I can't pretend not
to see doubled, not to see perfectly real on
each side of the glass. It has me standing
for a moment nowhere.

1986

The Bridge Is Gone

i

The great roar, the noise we travel in;
the bus swaying in the force of it,
in the black, along the difficult road
through Verdun. The sign makes it a name like others.
I imagine the land to have healed even its scars,
but they persist. The sky is abruptly lit
with the disfigured ghosts of the old dead.
We cross the Meuse, which remains the conduit
of their blood. It seems here we can't write it out,
the past is final.

In Nancy I thought I saw a sign
'La Maison de la Vie Claire'.
I'm told Giotto painted the clear,
uninterrupted look exchanged between God and Adam,
a look that went simply from one place to another,
that was as good as its word.
Seeing the Cimabue Madonna and Child
at the Louvre, I think I know that in it
God is lost, the Virgin's eyes, Christ's,
the Saint's, the Angels', none of them,
all of them looking askance,
they are looking towards nowhere.

By the Meuse, the trenches are unhealed
in my look, the insurrection of the dead.

The thud of the wipers is like a fist
pounding slowly against the screen.
This is a thing I'm afraid of:
sound that has no meaning.

ii

The wind continues.
For three days the building is restless
under its hand. The masonry will ride it out.
Every day I'm stronger.
The city rises around me:

the human mind, the human hand.
I didn't know I would die.
Now I have a sign,
I have something I can't leave behind.
What do I have to look at?
Not a building, not a piece of bread
or a tree.

I watch the tv news in relaxed
incomprehension until the famine pictures.
Out of my death I construct the imaginary
weight of their hunger, I flesh out
the indescribable, wordless arms. We want to live.

iii

The summer spent near the sound of waves
I sometimes heard and sometimes didn't hear.
A sound like breath, like stuttering,
running, the sound of the end of the world.
In what way is their voice understandable;
what do those steady syllables mean
beyond the anything we want them to mean?
Beyond that, they are their own,
are what they are outside of you,
subject to impersonal, inhuman laws
the human mind can't help bending to suit its own.

I sit dry on boulders left by some huge, geographic past.
Paper covers rock. I sit and drily watch
a small, droll bird I think of as a sandpiper
occupy itself at the water's margin.
Brimming with random intention, its life is full;
it keeps getting its feet wet.

Scissors cut paper. The bridge is gone,
its length only the length of our need,
and things sit disconnected side by side,
discrete. The sandpiper lifts each leg—
even in the absence of structure,
the insistent gift of vision.

And it's mine, that bird. *Rock breaks.*
Refraction close-crops the outline I need,
bending its intention to suit my hopes:
that the past—some tidal, particular past—is not final,
that there is escape, not from death,
but from the inability to live.

1986

ERIN MOURÉ
b. 1955

Vision Of a Woman Hit By a Bird

The flutter in my blood after the bird hit, as if
I would fall too,
head-on
into my throat, a soft body shaking its wings
& fallen
past me, the shock of it, its fury

at my chest unseen,
as if the bird had nested in me, that quickly.

Always now I am the woman hit by a bird.
I stand without emblem & defer
to my companions, their maleness & femininity,
their dress is a strangeness without purity;
I can't show them
my memory of the path under the trees
where I ran & was hit by the bird,
its brown eye, sincerely,
the blurred flight too late to stop
hitting my neck, then diving unhurt past me

Its mark is on my skin, a thin scrawl
invisible to medicine,
the bird's look in me, a hole,
sensible
Now I see the world thru my chest without asking,
as if I had the bird's eyes & bone flotation,

the earth's axis tipped,
spun away from the humans with their doctors' faces

The bird's stain I bandage on me,
heroically,
not like an emblem,
as if it were still the size & weight of a bird,
transubstantial,
its body on my throat with a flutter,
inexcusable surely,
my temperature at long last,
my melting point.

1985

Glow

Sitting in the old glow of summer, elbows
hunched over knees,
a bone marker in the green yard, clothed:
In the sun the body gives up its drugs
for stories.
The trees have run to the edge of the clearing, trampling their
    leaves.
They wait, tipped over, burnished, alive.

In the kitchen the kettle has boiled dry, the children lance long cries
into the yard.
Still the body sits, empty, staring dull eyes at the wood's edge.

Far away the branches tremble, tear their heart—
beat thru the air.
Desire creeps back to the body like a dog.
Children run from the house, the door bangs, somewhere
a key clicks in the ignition of a car.
Even the children, like trees, stand back from the body,
which hunches silently.
It touches their shadows with its hand.
Then stands up, a bone marker facing the yard.
'Once,' the body begins, talking softly, raising & lowering its
arms, white semaphore, its voice bending over & over,
pushes the years down.

Its life has been the death of many, today the body knows
what the pain was,
& how much it cost, & how many others
broke down crying & admitted everything: subversion, forbidden
    papers,
the knives.
The body looks around, the children play quietly away from it,
when it gets old, it knows they will not come.
It dreams of the last days it will spend, in bed,
stuck with tubing, the voices loud.

Even now the body knows, a bone marker in the glow of summer,
the trees halted impossibly   out of reach,
the children   impossibly   far & immune to calling
The body   already wise   stands & falters in need of its drug

1985

Philosophy of Language

A certain level of noise, the ear's false anguish, period.
She is reading a book, to herself, the
noise of this.
Huge rustling shakes the trees.
The windows fall open & lunge three stories downward
in a pirouette, ready for suicide.
A man stands up before her,
for all his height he is no taller than her shoe.
It is the inventor of the hinge.
He wants her to praise him
for inventing it.
When she leans forward the noise of the book
blows him over.

He wants her to love him, that's all.
But he shuts her out, waving the god–damn
almighty
root of language.
For all his bellow, he is no more agile
than a verb.
For all his pirouette, he is no regeneration.
He is no earth & no simile.

When she leans her woman-being toward him, he is
no name.
She is her simple rustling, shakes him, utterly,
without syndical perfection,
without period

1985

Gale Force

In your mouth my sentence begins
to say *sentence*
as if there were no more quaver
in the air between our mouths
& our speeches were all invented
at the end of a railway platform in the weeds
Now part of our body, my breast touches
sentence under the skin,
between our mouths, folding
Force of sentence

In your mouth my sentence opens, kissing you with its noise,
where I am no longer sleeping
where the railway has ended & waves loosely
in the heat risen up between the weeds
I dream
two women in the strange yard washing the trees,
having washed each single tree
it is daylight;
the wrung-out rags spread on their shoulders
to dry
Our tough reusable wings

In your mouth my sentence is periodically sentence,
my skin crying short uttered joy:

it is out loud

it is out noise

it is over there & here

Heat risen past us, *gale force*, the trees
shining bright in the yard,
between our bodies,   pale wings,   & the railway

1985

Aspen

Woman whose arms are the bones of the poem,
full of indispensable marrow

Her mouth is a lone cry behind
an aspen, the weeds grown tangled, cow parsnip, brown canes of
raspberry, sunlight,
I touch her with my mouth

& our two cries flutter,
impossible havoc, heat, haven, have–not of the body,
our tensions in its arms & folded openings in its centre,
where we touch the cry
without knowing its sense
finally
deep inside the marrow
Hushed in each other for a moment, the leaves still

before we separate
& it begins again, each cry
behind its aspen, each aspen
clattering its leaves in sunlight, dropping silver onto the floor

1988

The Producers

What the producers do to meat, you pay for in your cells,
It is your cells I have come to speak about.
Only a certain thickness separates me from the air in this room.
Density. Its whirligig spinning
to the tune of bouzouki music.
My body the street fair offers you the altered clothing of the cells.
It offers you the chance to read a novel by a famous woman

in which other women reproduce, & their
value is this:
reproduction.

It is because of this I have come to speak to you:
because it is possible that
the meaning of a woman is the meaning of a single cell.

A certain thickness prevents me from saying what I might say.
The difference between a human cell & the atoms in this table.
I lean my head against the wood.
Where are you, I want to speak to you.
What the producers do to lettuce, you pay for in your cells.
Everything they do, you will pay for.
Your cells will not recognize what they are to become.
It is on behalf of your cells.
I speak to you without election because the cells know nothing
of democracy.
They think not of the good of the whole, but of themselves.
They think of their thin unguarded border.
The illusion of wholeness captivates us, as a kind of slavery.
I asked a woman with cancer, who told me.
Now she has died because some cells wanted to go
someplace else.
Before she died, she thought about the producers
of x-rays,
& how we once believed we could see thru anything,
we humans.

1988

ANNE MICHAELS
b. 1958

Lake of Two Rivers

I

Pull water, unhook its seam.

Lie down in the lake room,
in the smell of leaves still sticky from their birth.

Fall to sleep the way the moon falls
from earth: perfect lethargy of orbit.

2

Six years old, half asleep,
a traveller. The night car mysterious
as we droned past uneasy twisting fields.

My father told two stories on these drives.
One was the plot of 'Lost Horizon',
the other: his life.
This speeding room, dim in the dashboard's green emission,
became the hijacked plane carrying Ronald Colman to Tibet,
or the train carrying my father across Poland in 1931.

Spirit faces crowded the windows of a '64 Buick.
Unknown cousins surrounded us, arms around each other,
a shawl of sleeves.

The moon fell into our car from Grodno.
It fell from Chaya-Elke's village,
where they stopped to say goodbye.
His cousin Mashka sat up with them
in the barn, while her face
floated down the River Neman in my father's guitar.
He watched to remember
in the embalming moonlight.

3

Sensate weather, we are your body,
your memory. Like a template,
branch defines sky, leaves
bleed their gritty boundaries,
corrosive with nostalgia.

Each year we go outside to pin it down,
light limited, light specific,
light like a name.

*

For years my parents fled at night,
loaded their children in the back seat,
a tangle of pyjamas anxious to learn the stars.

I watched the backs of their heads
until I was asleep, and when I woke
it was day, and we were in Algonquin.

I've always known this place,
familiar as a room in our house.

The photo of my mother, legs locked in water,
looking into the hills where you and I stand—

only now do I realize
it was taken before I was born.

*

Purple mist, indefinite hills.

At Two Rivers, close as branches.
Fish scatter, silver pulses with their own electric logic.

Milky spill of moon over the restless lake,
seen through a sieve of foliage.

In fields to the south
vegetables radiate underground,
displace the earth.
While we sit, linked by firelight.

4

The longer you look at a thing
the more it transforms.

My mother's story is tangled,
overgrown with lives of parents and grandparents
because they lived in one house and among them
remembered hundreds of years of history.

This domestic love is plain, hurts
the way light balancing objects in a still life hurts.

The heart keeps body and spirit in suspension,
until density pulls them apart.
When she was my age
her mother had already fallen through.

Pregnant, androgynous with man,
she was afraid. When life goes out,
loss gets in, wedging a new place.

Under dark lanes of the night sky
the eyes of our skin won't close,
we dream in desire.

Love wails from the womb, caldera, home.
Like any sound, it goes on forever.

*

The dissolving sun turns Two Rivers into skin.
Our pink arms, slightly fluorescent,
hiss in the dusky room, neon tubes bending
in the accumulated dark.

Night transforms the lake into a murmuring solid.
Naked in the eerie tremor of leaves rubbing stars,
in the shivering fermata of summer,
in the energy of stones made powerful by gravity,
desire made powerful by the seam between starlight and skin,
we join, moebius ribbon in the night room.

5

We do not descend, but rise from our histories.
If cut open memory would resemble
a cross-section of the earth's core,
a table of geographical time.
Faces press the transparent membrane
between conscious and genetic knowledge.
A name, a word, triggers the dilation.
Motive is uncovered, sharp overburden in a shifting field.

*

When I was twenty-five I drowned in the River Neman,
fell through when I read that bone-black from the ovens
was discarded there.

Like a face pressed against a window,
part of you waits up for them,
like a parent, you wait up.

*

A family now, we live each other's life
without the details.

The forest flies apart, trees are shaken loose
by my tears,

by love that doesn't fall to earth
but bursts up from the ground, fully formed.

1985

Rain Makes Its Own Night

Rain makes its own night, long mornings with lamps left on.
Lean beach grass sticks to the floor near your shoes,
last summer's pollen rises from damp metal screens.

This is order, this clutter that fills clearings between us,
clothes clinging to chairs, your shoes in a muddy grip.

The hard rain smells like it comes from the earth.
The human light in our windows, the orange stillness
of rooms seen from outside. The place we fall to alone,
falling to sleep. Surrounded by a forest's green assurance,
the iron gauze of sky and sea,
while night, the rain, pulls itself down through the trees.

1985

BIOGRAPHIES

MARGARET ATWOOD was born in Ottawa in 1939. In addition to such novels as *Lady Oracle* (1976) and *The Handmaid's Tale* (1986), she has published over ten books of poetry, including *The Circle Game* (1966), which won a Governor General's Award, *The Journals of Susanna Moodie* (1970), *Power Politics* (1973), *Selected Poems* (1976), *True Stories* (1981), *Interlunar* (1981), *Murder in the Dark* (1983), and *Selected Poems II: Poems Selected and New 1976-1986* (1986).

MARGARET AVISON was born in Galt, Ont., in 1918. Her books include *Winter Sun* (1960), which won a Governor General's Award, *The Dumbfounding* (1966), and *Sunblue* (1978).

MARGARET BLENNERHASSET was born in Ireland in 1778 and came to Montreal in 1819. She is known to have published one book, *The Widow of the Rock and Other Poems* (1824).

JEAN BLEWETT was born at Scotia, Lake Erie, Ont., in 1872. A popular poet in her day, she is the author of *Heart Songs* (1897), *The Cornflower and Other Poems* (1906), and *Jean Blewett's Poems* (1922).

ROO BORSON was born in Berkeley, Calif., in 1952, and moved to Canada in 1972. Her books include *Landfall* (1977), *In the Smoky Light of the Fields* (1980), *Rain* (1980), *A Sad Device* (1981), and *The Whole Night, Coming Home* (1984).

MARILYN BOWERING was born in Winnipeg in 1949. Her works include *The Liberation of Newfoundland* (1973), *The Killing Room* (1977), *The Visitors Have All Returned* (1979), *Sleeping with Lambs* (1980), *Giving Back Diamonds* (1982), *The Sunday Before Winter* (1984), *Anyone Can See I Love You* (1987), and *Winter Harbour: Selected Poetry* (1987).

LOUISE MOREY BOWMAN was born in Sherbrooke, Que., in 1882. Published widely in Canada and the U.S., her imagist poems won the admiration of Amy Lowell and Harriet Monroe. Her works include *Moonlight and Common Day* (1922), *Dream Tapestries* (1924), and *Characters in Cadence* (1938).

DIONNE BRAND was born in Trinidad in 1953 and came to Canada in 1970. Her books include *'Fore Day Morning* (1979), *Earth Magic* (1980), *Primitive Offensive* (1982), *Winter Epigrams & Epigrams to Ernesto Cardenal in Defense of Claudia* (1983), and *Chronicles of the Hostile Sun* (1984).

ELIZABETH BREWSTER was born in Chipman, N.B., in 1922. Her books of poetry include *Passage of Summer* (1969), *Sunrise North* (1972), *In Search of Eros* (1974), *Poems* (1977), *The Way Home* (1982), and *Digging* (1982), as well as several works of fiction.

AUDREY ALEXANDRA BROWN was born in Nanaimo, B.C. in 1904. Her five volumes of poetry include *A Dryad in Nanaimo* (1931), *Challenge to Time and Death* (1943), and *All Fools' Day* (1948).

SKYROS BRUCE is a Salishan poet. Her book *Kalala Poems* was published by Daylight Press in 1972.

JAN CONN was born in the Eastern Townships, Que., in 1952. Her books include *Red Shoes in the Rain* (1984) and *The Fabulous Disguise of Ourselves* (1986).

JENI COUZYN was born in South Africa in 1942 and came to Canada in 1973. Her works include *Flying* (1970), *Monkey's Wedding* (1972), *Christmas in Africa* (1975), *House of Changes* (1978), and *Life by Drowning* (1983; rev. edn, 1985). She is the editor of *The Bloodaxe Book of Contemporary Women Poets* (1985). She currently lives in England.

ISABELLA VALANCY CRAWFORD was born in Dublin in 1850 and immigrated to Canada in 1858. Although she published a great many short stories and novelettes, mainly in American magazines, her reputation rests on the poems published in *Old Spookses' Pass, Malcolm's Katie, and Other Poems* (1884).

LORNA CROZIER was born in Swift Current, Sask., in 1948. Her books include *Inside is the Sky* (1976), *Crow's Black Joy* (1978), *Humans and Other Beasts* (1980), *The Weather* (1983), and *The Garden Going On Without Us* (1985).

MARY DI MICHELE was born in Italy in 1949 and immigrated with her family in 1955. Her books include *Tree of August* (1978), *Bread and Chocolate* (1980), *Mimosa and Other Poems* (1981), *Necessary Sugar* (1984), and *Immune to Gravity* (1986).

ANNIE CHARLOTTE DALTON was born at Birkby, Huddersfield, Eng., in 1865 and moved to Vancouver in 1904. Her writing career began in Canada. Her works include *The Marriage of Music* (1910) and *Flame and Adventure* (1924).

GWLADYS DOWNES was born in Victoria, B.C., in 1915. Her books include *Lost Diver* (1955), *When We Lie Together* (1973), and *Out of the Violent Dark* (1978).

JUDITH FITZGERALD was born in Toronto in 1952. Her books of poetry include *City Park* (1972), *Victory* (1975), *Lacerating Heartwood* (1977), *Easy Over* (1981), *Split/Levels* (1983), *The Syntax of Things* (1984), *Beneath the Skin of Paradise: The Piaf Poems* (1984), *Given Names* (1985), and *Diary of Desire* (1987).

GAIL FOX was born in Willimantic, Conn., in 1942. Her books include *Dangerous Seasons* (1969), *The Royal Collector of Dreams* (1970), *The Ringmaster's Circus* (1973), *Flight of the Pterodactyl* (1973), *God's Odd Look* (1976), *In Search of Living Things* (1980), *Houses of God* (1983), and *The Deepening of the Colours* (1986).

SUSAN GLICKMAN was born in Baltimore, Md, in 1953 and grew up in Montreal. Her books include *Complicity* (1983) and *The Power to Move* (1987).

PHYLLIS GOTLIEB was born in Toronto in 1926. Although she has gained her reputation for her novels (mostly science fiction), verse-dramas, and short stories, she has published a number of books of poetry, including *Who Knows One* (1961), *Within the Zodiac* (1964), *Ordinary, Moving* (1969), *Doctor Umlaut's Earthly Kingdom* (1974), and *The Works* (1978).

ELIZABETH GOURLAY was born in Toronto in 1917 and is both a playwright and a poet. Her works include the plays *Isabel* (1979), *The Glass Bottle* (1981), and *No Recourse* (1984), and the poetry collections *Motions, Dreams And Aberrations* (1969), *Songs and Dances* (1981), and *M Poems* (1983).

KRISTJANA GUNNARS was born in Iceland in 1948 and came to Canada in 1969. Among her books are *Settlement Poems 1 and 2* (1980), *One-Eyed Moon Maps* (1981), *Wake-Pick Poems* (1982), *The Axe's Edge* (1983), and *The Night Workers of Ragnarok* (1985).

KATHERINE HALE (Amelia Beers Garvin) was born in Galt, Ont., in 1887. She worked as a journalist and in 1912 was elected President of the Women's Press Club. She published over seven books, including *Grey Knitting* (1914), *The White Comrade* (1916), and *The New Joan* (1917).

DIANA HARTOG was born in California in 1942 and immigrated to Canada in 1971. She has published two books of poetry: *Matinee Light* (1983), which won the Gerald Lampert Award for the best achievement by a new Canadian poet, and *Candy From Strangers* (1986).

CLAIRE HARRIS was born in Trinidad and came to Canada in 1966. Her books include *Fables from the Women's Quarters* (1984), *Translation into Fiction* (1984), and *Travelling to Find a Remedy* (1986).

SUSIE FRANCES HARRISON was born in Toronto in 1859. She was a professional pianist and vocalist and an authority on French-Canadian folksongs. Though she wrote two novels, a play, and short stories, she was best known as a poet. Her most ambitious collection is *Pine, Rose, and Fleur de Lis* (1891).

PAULETTE JILES was born in Missouri in 1943 and came to Canada in 1969. Her work includes *Waterloo Express* (1973), *The Golden Hawks* (1978), *Celestial Navigation* (1984), which won a Governor General's Award, *Sitting in the Club Car Drinking Rum and Karma-Kola* (1986), *The Late Great Human Road Show* (1986), and *The James Poems* (1987).

E. PAULINE JOHNSON was born on the Six Nations Reserve near Brantford, Ont., in 1861, the daughter of a Mohawk father and an English mother. Extremely popular as a performer, she toured North America and England, finding an enthusiastic audience for her poetry. Her works include *Legends of Vancouver* (1911) and *Flint and Feather* (1912).

JANICE KULYK KEEFER was born in Toronto in 1952. Her published work includes the novel *The Paris-Napoli Express* (1986) and a book of poetry, *White of the Lesser Angels* (1986).

JOY KOGAWA was born in Vancouver in 1935 and is best known for her novel *Obasan* (1981). Her books of poetry include *The Splintered Moon* (1968), *A Choice of Dreams* (1974), *Jericho Road* (1978), and *Woman in the Woods* (1985).

DOROTHY LIVESAY was born in Winnipeg in 1909. She has been a major force in Canadian literature, publishing over fifteen books of prose and poetry. As an editor she has been influential in establishing the shape of Canadian poetry. Her works include *Collected Poems: The Two Seasons* (1972), *The Self-Completing Tree: Selected Poems* (1986), and *A Winnipeg Childhood* (1975).

PAT LOWTHER was born in Vancouver in 1935. Before her death in 1975 she published three books of poetry: *This Difficult Flowering* (1968), *The Age of the Bird* (1972), and *Milk Stone* (1974). *A Stone Diary* was published posthumously in 1976.

GWENDOLYN MacEWEN was born in Toronto in 1941. Though she published two novels as well as several collections of short stories and a travelogue, she is best known for her books of poetry, which include *A Breakfast for Barbarians* (1966), *The Shadow-Maker* (1969), winner of a Governor General's Award, *Magic Animals: Selected Poems Old and New* (1974), *The T.E. Lawrence Poems* (1982), *Earth Light: Selected Poetry* (1982) and *Afterworlds* (1987), which also won a Governor General's Award.

JAY MACPHERSON was born in England in 1931. She came to Canada as a child and now lives in Toronto. Her work includes *The Boatman* (1957), which won a Governor General's Award, *Welcoming Disaster* (1974), and *Poems Twice Told* (1981). *Four Ages of Man: The Classical Myths* (1962) is a retelling of myths for young people.

FLORIS CLARKE McLAREN was born in 1904 and lives in Victoria, B.C. One of the founding editors of *Contemporary Verse,* she published one book of poetry, *Frozen Fire* (1937).

DAPHNE MARLATT was born in Melbourne, Australia, in 1942, and came to Canada in 1951. Her books of poetry include *leaf leaf/s* (1969), *Rings* (1971), *Vancouver Poems* (1972), *Steveston* (1974), *Net Work: Selected Writing* (1980), *What Matters* (1980), *Here and There* (1981), *How Hug a Stone* (1983), and *Touch to My Tongue* (1984).

ANNE MARRIOTT was born in Victoria, B.C., in 1913. She was on the founding committee of *Contemporary Verse.* Her books include *Calling Adventurers* (1941), for which she won a Governor General's Award, *Sandstone and Other Poems* (1945), *Countries* (1971), and *The Circular Coast: New and Selected Poems* (1981).

ANNE MICHAELS was born in Toronto in 1958. Her first book of poetry, *The Weight of Oranges,* was published in 1985.

LUCY MAUD MONTGOMERY was born at Clifton (now New London), P.E.I., in 1874. Best known for her novel *Anne of Green Gables* (1908) and its sequels, she published more than twenty books, including the *The Watchman and Other Poems* (1916).

SUSANNA MOODIE was born in Suffolk, England, and immigrated to Canada in 1832. The author of *Roughing it in the Bush: or, Life in Canada* (1852), she published widely in the Canadian and British magazines of her time.

ERIN MOURÉ was born in Calgary in 1955. Her books include *Empire, York Street* (1979), *The Whisky Vigil* (1982), *Wanted Alive* (1983), *Domestic Fuel* (1985), and *Furious* (1988).

RONA MURRAY was born in London, England, in 1924 and came to Canada in 1932. Her work includes *The Enchanted Adder* (1965), The Power of the Dog (1968), *Selected Poems* (1974), *Journey* (1982), and *Adam and Eve in Middle Age* (1984).

SUSAN MUSGRAVE was born in 1951 in California and grew up in British Columbia. Her books of poetry include *Songs of the Sea-Witch* (1970), *Entrance of the Celebrant* (1972), *Grave-Dirt and Selected Strawberries* (1973), *The Impstone* (1976), *Selected Strawberries and Other Poems* (1977), *A Man to Marry, A Man to Bury* (1979), *Tarts and Muggers* (1982), and *Cocktails at the Mausoleum* (1985).

MARTHA OSTENSO was born near Bergen, Norway, in 1900 and came with her family to North America in 1902. They moved to Brandon, Man., and then to Winnipeg, which provides the background for her most important novel, *Wild Geese* (1925). She published over a dozen volumes of fiction and a collection of poetry: *A Far Land* (1924).

P.K. PAGE was born at Swanage, in the south of England, in 1917; her family immigrated to Canada in 1919. Among her best-known works are *The Metal and the Flower* (1954), which won a Governor General's Award, *Cry Ararat: Poems New and Selected* (1967), *The Glass Air: Selected Poems* (1985), and *Brazilian Journal* (1987).

MARLENE NOURBESE PHILIP was born in Tobago in 1947 and immigrated to Canada in 1968. Her works include *Thorns* (1980), *Salmon Courage* (1983), the novel *Harriet's Daughter* (1988), and *She Tries Her Tongue* (1988).

MARJORIE PICKTHALL was born in Gunnersby, Middlesex, England, in 1883 and immigrated to Canada in 1889. Her reputation as a poet, considerable in her day, rests on two volumes: *The Drift of Pinions* (1913) and *The Lamp of Poor Souls* (1916), as well as *The Complete Poems of Marjorie Pickthall* (1925), a posthumous collection compiled by her father.

DOROTHY ROBERTS was born in Fredericton, N.B., in 1906. Her books include *Dazzle* (1957), *In Star and Stalk* (1959), *Twice to Flame* (1961), *Extended* (1976), and *The Self of Loss: New and Selected Poems* (1976).

ROBYN SARAH was born in New York in 1949 to Canadian parents. Her works include *Shadowplay* (1978), *The Space Between Sleep and Waking* (1981), *Anyone Skating on the Middle Ground* (1984), and *Becoming Light* (1987).

LIBBY SCHEIER was born in New York City in 1946 and came to Canada in 1975. Her works include *The Larger Life* (1983) and *Second Nature* (1986).

CAROLYN SMART was born in England in 1952 and came to Canada as a child. Her books include *Swimmers in Oblivion* (1981), *Power Sources* (1982), and *Stoning the Moon* (1986).

ELIZABETH SMART was born in Ottawa in 1913 and is best known for her novels *By Grand Central Station I Sat Down and Wept* (1945) and *The Assumption of Rogues and Rascals* (1978). Her poetry includes A Bonus (1977), *Eleven Poems* (1982), and *In the Meantime: A Collection of Poetry and Prose* (1985).

KAY SMITH was born in Saint John, N.B., in 1911. Her books include *Footnote to the Lord's Prayer and Other Poems* (1951), *At the Bottom of the Dark* (1971), *When a Girl Looks Down* (1978), *White Paper Face in the Window* (1987), and *The Bright Particulars: Poems Selected and New* (1987).

ROSEMARY SULLIVAN was born in Montreal in 1947. Her collection of poems *The Space a Name Makes* (1986) won the Gerald Lampert Award for the best achievement by a new poet.

ANNE SZUMIGALSKI was born in London, England, in 1926 and came to Canada in 1955. Her works include *Woman Reading in Bath* (1974), *A Game of Angels* (1980), *Doctrine of Signatures* (1983), *Risks* (1983), and *Dogstones: Selected and New Poems* (1986).

SHARON THESEN was born in Tisdale, Sask., in 1946. Her work includes *Artemis Hates Romance* (1980), *Holding the Pose* (1983), and *The Beginning of the Long Dash* (1987).

COLLEEN THIBAUDEAU was born in Toronto in 1935. Her books include *Lozenges: Poems in the Shape of Things* (1965), *Ten Letters* (1975), *My Granddaughters Are Combing Out Their Long Hair* (1977), and *The Martha Landscapes* (1984).

LOLA LEMIRE TOSTEVIN was born in Timmins, Ont., in 1937. Her works include *Color of Her Speech* (1982), *Gyno-Text* (1983), *Double Standards* (1985), and *'sophie* (1988).

RHEA TREGEBOV was born in Saskatoon in 1953. Her works include *Remembering History* (1982), which won the Pat Lowther Prize, and *No One We Know* (1986).

KATE VAN DUSEN was born in Ottawa in 1952. Her books include *Black Shoes* (1983) and *Not Noir* (1987).

PAMELIA VINING YULE was born in Clarendon, N.Y., in 1825. Author of *Poems of the Heart and Home* (1881) and several prose works, she died in Ingersoll, Ont., in 1896.

MARIAM WADDINGTON was born in Winnipeg in 1917. While pursuing a career in social work and as a Professor of English at York University, she published over twelve books, including *The Price of Gold* (1976), *The Visitants* (1981), and *Collected Poems* (1986).

BRONWEN WALLACE was born in Kingston, Ont., in 1945. Her books include *Signs of the Former Tenant* (1983), *Common Magic* (1985), and *The Stubborn Particulars of Grace* (1987).

PHYLLIS WEBB was born in Vancouver, B.C., in 1927. Her works include *Trio* (1954), *Even Your Right Eye* (1956), *The Sea Is Also A Garden* (1962), *Naked Poems* (1965), *Selected Poems 1954-1965* (1971), *Wilson's Bowl* (1980), *Selected Poems: The Vision Tree* (1982), which won a Governor General's Award, and *Water and Light: Ghazals and Anti Ghazals* (1984). One of the most sophisticated of Canadian poets, she has her critical writings and thoughts on the creative process in *Talking* (1982).

ANNE WILKINSON was born in Toronto in 1910. Although she is best known for her two books of poetry, *Counterpoint to Sleep* (1951) and *The Hangman Ties the Holly* (1955), she was also accomplished in prose, as can be seen in *Lions in the Way* (1956), in which she traced her family history. *The Collected Poems of Anne Wilkinson* was published in 1968.

ADELE WISEMAN was born in Winnipeg in 1928. She is best known for her prose works, including *The Sacrifice* (1956), which won a Governor General's Award, *Crackpot* (1974), and *Old Woman at Play* (1978). A Collection of her essays, *Memoirs of A Book-Molesting Childhood*, appeared in 1987.

INDEX OF POETS